RELYING ON THE

HOLY SPIRIT

BY

CHARLES F. STANLEY

THOMAS NELSON
Since 1798

Published in Nashville, Tennessee, by Thomas Nelson, Inc., Publishers, and distributed in Canada by Word Communications, Ltd., Richmond, British Columbia.

Editing, layout, and design by Gregory C. Benoit Publishing, Old Mystic, CT

ISBN 1-4185-3336-X

Printed in the United States of America

10 11 WC 10 9

Contents

Why We Need the Holy Spirit

All Christians have had an experience with the Holy Spirit—otherwise, they really aren't Christians. For a proper understanding of who the Holy Spirit is and how He works in our lives, we must go to God's Word. We can't base our relationship with the Holy Spirit on feelings or experiences.

Some people have been taught erroneously about the Holy Spirit. I know people who have taken one verse out of the Bible and built an entire theology of the Holy Spirit on it. We must have the whole counsel of God's Word on the subject of the Holy Spirit if we hope to have a full understanding of Him and a fuller experience with Him.

As in all areas of study, we err if we base our believing on one isolated concept. Truth in God's Word is expressed repeatedly. Verses build upon verses to create the whole meaning of God's message to us. Our perspective is limited—and in error—unless we take in the whole of God's truth.

This book can be used by you alone or by several people in a small-group study. At various times, you will be asked to relate to the material in one of these four ways:

1. *What new insights have you gained?* Make notes about the insights that you have. You may want to record them in your Bible or in a separate journal. As you reflect back over your insights, you are likely to see how God has moved in your life.

2. *Have you ever had a similar experience?* Each of us approaches the Bible from a unique background—our own particular set of relationships and experiences. Our experiences do not make the Bible true—the Word of God is truth regardless of our opinion about it. It is important, however, to share our experiences in order to see how God's truth can be applied to human lives.

3. *How do you feel about the material presented?* Emotional responses do not give validity to the Scriptures, nor should we trust our emotions as a gauge for our faith. In small-group Bible study, however, it is good for participants to express their emotions. The Holy Spirit often communicates with us through this unspoken language.

4. *In what way do you feel challenged to respond or to act?* God's Word may cause you to feel inspired or challenged to change something in your life. Take the challenge seriously and find ways of acting upon it. If God reveals to you a particular need that He wants *you* to address, take that as "marching orders" from God. God is expecting you to *do* something with the challenge that He has just given you.

Start and conclude your Bible study sessions in prayer. Ask God to give you spiritual eyes to see and spiritual ears to hear. As you conclude your study, ask the Lord to seal what you have learned so that you will never forget it. Ask Him to help you grow into the fullness of the stature of Christ Jesus.

Again, I caution you to keep the Bible at the center of your study. A genuine Bible study stays focused on God's Word and promotes a growing faith and a closer walk with the Holy Spirit in *each* person who participates.

The Spirit-Filled Life is for Every Believer

❧ In This Lesson ❧

LEARNING: WHAT DOES THE PHRASE "SPIRIT-FILLED LIFE" ACTUALLY MEAN?

GROWING: WHO CAN HAVE A SPIRIT-FILLED LIFE?

In all likelihood, the words "Spirit-filled life" evoke one of three responses in you. You may say, "I don't know what you're talking about." If that's your response, you aren't alone. Many people don't know much about the Holy Spirit, and they know less about how He works in the life of every Christian.

You may say, "I'm not sure that I want anything to do with the Holy Spirit. Everything that I've heard about the Holy Spirit seems divisive or too emotional for me." If that's your response, I have encouragement for you. If you are a born-again Christian, you have a relationship with the Holy Spirit, whether you have acknowledged Him or not. Furthermore, *He* is not divisive or invasive. People may be, but He is not.

You may say, "Oh, yes! The Spirit-filled life is the most wonderful life that a person can know. I wouldn't trade the Spirit-filled life for all the riches in the world or for any other experience!" If that's your response, I say "amen"—so be it. The Spirit-filled life is the only way for a Christian to experience all that God wants us to be, say, and do. It is life to the fullest, the true abundant life that Jesus promised. (See John 10:10.)

The Spirit-filled life is not based on emotions, although you are likely to feel various emotions as the Spirit works in you to produce the character of Christ Jesus and to replicate the ministry of Christ Jesus in your life and the world. The Spirit-filled life is also not something that a person can study from afar. The Spirit-filled life is experienced. It is lived out by real people in real life facing real, and sometimes difficult, circumstances and situations.

The Spirit-filled life is marked by purpose, power, and effectiveness. It is not something that you *do*, but something that you *are* because of who is living and working inside you. God wants each of His children to live a Spirit-filled life, and He expects you to be led by the Spirit on a daily basis.

Why do I need the Holy Spirit?

Most of us have no difficulty admitting, "I need Jesus Christ in my life." We recognize that we are sinful creatures by nature and that we must have the all-sufficient atonement made possible by Christ Jesus on the cross if we are to experience forgiveness for our sins and to receive eternal life. Most of us have no difficulty admitting, "I need God the Father in my life." We recognize Him as our all-powerful, ever-present, and holy Creator. Jesus Christ came into the world so that we might be restored to a full relationship with our heavenly Father, who desires to bless us as His children. In many ways, we need Christ Jesus in our lives because of our need for a relationship with the Father.

But do we need the Holy Spirit? The Holy Spirit is part of the holy Trinity—Father, Son, and Holy Spirit. You need Him just as much as you need Father and Son. In fact, the Holy Spirit makes possible your ongoing Christian life and enables you to experience Christ and to have a relationship with the Father. The Holy Spirit enables you to have victory in your Christian walk. You need Him at work in you if you are to fulfill your earthly destiny in Christ and become the person that the Father created you to be.

Beyond Adequate

Many Christians are content to live an adequate Christian life. They believe that if they go to church, read their Bible occasionally, and say their prayers once in a while, they are alright with God. Occasionally, they volunteer to serve others in a particular way—perhaps as an usher, a member of a church committee, or a home visitor on an evangelism team—and they consider that ministry as above the norm.

Let me challenge you today. God doesn't call you or anyone to just an adequate Christian life. He wants to have a daily walking-and-talking relationship with you in which you experience His presence, trust Him for wisdom, courage, and strength, and rely on Him for results—at every step you take, every decision you make, every conversation you have, and every thought you think. The Lord desires to live within you. He desires to communicate to you and through you. He desires to live out His life through your expression of it—a perfect blending of His perfection and your unique talents, traits, and personality.

There is no such thing as an average Christian life. Either you are living a vibrant Spirit-filled life, or you aren't. You are in forward motion or in a pause position. You are living in the fullness of the Holy Spirit, or you aren't. Make a decision today to choose the Spirit-filled life. God will not force Himself on you or force Himself to operate within you. He works by invitation only. He won't overstep the boundaries of your will.

Lay Aside Your Preconceptions

You probably have some preconceptions about the Holy Spirit and how He works within a person's life. I encourage you to lay them aside and approach these lessons with a wide-open heart and mind. You can learn and experience something here—but only if you are willing to be changed in your inner person.

> But the Helper, the Holy Spirit, whom the Father will send in My name, He will teach you all things, and bring to your remembrance all things that I said to you.
>
> —John 14:26

❧ When you hear the phrase "Spirit-filled life," what comes to your mind?

❧ Are you open to knowing and experiencing more of the Holy Spirit in your life?

Do you want more out of your relationship with Christ Jesus than you are currently experiencing?

Today and Tomorrow

TODAY: THE HOLY SPIRIT DWELLS WITHIN THE LIFE OF EVERY CHRISTIAN.

TOMORROW: I WILL STUDY THE SCRIPTURES THIS WEEK TO LEARN MORE ABOUT THE HOLY SPIRIT.

Notes and Prayer Requests:

LESSON 2

Who Exactly is the Holy Spirit?

---- ❧ **In This Lesson** ❧ ----

LEARNING: IS THE HOLY SPIRIT A PERSON OR SOME OTHER ENTITY?

GROWING: IF THE HOLY SPIRIT IS A PERSON, WHAT DOES THAT MEAN TO ME?

Have you ever seen a child stare in wide-eyed wonder as he listens to a new story? That's the way many people are when it comes to the Holy Spirit. They don't have a clue to His true identity or how He works in the life of every Christian. The Holy Spirit is a mystery to them.

Wide-eyed wonder is not a bad response to have to the Holy Spirit. Certainly, the Holy Spirit should inspire our awe, our wonder, our adoration. But He does not want to be a puzzle. He desires to reveal Himself to us and to be known by us. Who, then, is the Holy Spirit? That's the focus of this lesson.

The Holy Spirit Is a Person

One of the keys to your understanding about the Holy Spirit lies in your recognition that the Holy Spirit is not an "it"; He is a person. Have you ever been asked, "Are you filled with the Holy Spirit? Do you have the Holy Spirit?" There is only one set of answers: yes or no. You can't have a little bit of the Holy Spirit. Either you have been filled by Him, or you haven't. You can't have had Him once, but not have Him now. Either you have Him, or you've never had Him.

The error tends to come because we think of the Holy Spirit as a force, a power, an event, an experience, a manifestation. I once had this view of the Holy Spirit. When I went to college to prepare for the ministry, the subject of the Holy Spirit came up in conversation. I must have referred to the Holy Spirit as "it," because at the end of that discussion, one man in the group asked me if I'd meet with him later in his dorm room. He was a graduate student in theology so I was honored at the invitation and I gladly accepted.

When I went to his room, I was amazed to find that the walls were lined entirely with books. I felt that I was in the presence of a true scholar. He handed me a Greek New Testament, and I have to say, I was dismayed. I admitted to him that I had been at the college only a couple of weeks and I scarcely knew more than a few words and phrases in Greek. That didn't deter him. He proceeded to go through the New Testament with me, one verse after another, teaching me that the Holy Spirit is not an "it" but a "He"—a person, a member of the holy Trinity. My entire perspective changed.

When you begin to see the Holy Spirit as a person—not as a power or an experience—you have a much different perspective on receiving the Holy Spirit. Where does our false understanding of the Holy Spirit as an "it" originate? In many cases, from Acts 2 where we read about the coming of the Holy Spirit into the lives of the first Christians:

> When the Day of Pentecost had fully come, they were all with one accord in one place. And suddenly there came a sound from heaven, as of a rushing mighty wind, and it filled the whole house where they were sitting. Then there appeared

9

to them divided tongues, as of fire, and one sat upon each of them. And they were all filled with the Holy Spirit and began to speak with other tongues, as the Spirit gave them utterance.

—Acts 2:1–4

People tend to confuse the sights and sounds present at the Holy Spirit's arrival with the Holy Spirit Himself. They read of a rushing wind-like sound from heaven. They read of a mass of fire that seems to divide into tongues that touch each person. They read of the people speaking in languages that they didn't learn with their minds, and they assume that the sound, the fire, and the unknown tongues are the Holy Spirit.

These are manifestations of the Spirit's coming to the church on the day of Pentecost shortly after Jesus' ascension. They are *not* the Holy Spirit Himself. The sound is *as* a rushing mighty wind. The glowing light seems *as* divided tongues of fire. The Holy Spirit is infinitely more than any single manifestation of His presence.

☙ Why were the disciples "all with one accord in one place" when the Holy Spirit came to them? What does this suggest about the Spirit's role in the church?

☙ Consider each of the manifestations of the Spirit's presence: wind, tongues of fire, speaking in foreign languages. What does each reveal about the Holy Spirit?

The Characteristics of a Person

What makes a human being different from any of God's other creatures? The three foremost qualities of humanity are these:

1. *Knowledge*—an ability to know, understand, recognize, and have meaning

2. *Will*—an ability to make choices and decisions on the basis of what one chooses to do, not as an instinctive response to external stimuli

3. *Emotion*—an ability to feel, to have feelings and to be aware of them

Let's take a look at Scriptures that reveal these qualities associated with the Holy Spirit.

We read about the *knowing* ability of the Holy Spirit: "For what man knows the things of a man except the spirit of the man which is in him? Even so no one knows the things of God except the Spirit of God" (1 Cor. 2:11).

And we read about the *will* of the Holy Spirit: "But one and the same Spirit works all these things, distributing to each one individually as He wills" (1 Cor. 12:11).

In Romans 15:30, we read about "the love of the Spirit," and in Ephesians 4:30, we read Paul's admonishment: "Do not grieve the Holy Spirit of God." We can't grieve Somebody who doesn't love us. We can grieve the Holy Spirit because He has an emotional capacity. Yes, the Holy Spirit has *emotions*.

11

And I will pray the Father, and He will give you another Helper, that He may abide with you forever—the Spirit of truth, whom the world cannot receive, because it neither sees Him nor knows Him; but you know Him, for He dwells with you and will be in you.

—John 14:16–17

∾ What words in these verses point to the fact that the Holy Spirit is a divine person?

∾ What roles of the Holy Spirit are listed in these verses?

The Holy Spirit Is Part of the Trinity

The Holy Spirit is the third member of the triune Godhead: God the Father, God the Son, and God the Holy Spirit. He is inseparable from the Father and the Son; He is of one nature, character, and identity with them. At the same time, He is a unique person; He has a specific identity and function in our lives, just as Jesus has a specific identity and function and the Father has a specific identity and function. The Holy Spirit is present whenever the Father and the Son are present, and they in turn are present whenever the Holy Spirit is present.

The Holy Spirit was present at creation: "The earth was without form, and void; and darkness was on the face of the deep. And the Spirit of God was hovering over the face of the waters" (Gen. 1:2). And He was vital in the creation of mankind:

> Then God said, "Let Us make man in Our image, according to Our likeness; let them have dominion over the fish of the sea, over the birds of the air, and over the cattle, over all the earth and over every creeping thing that creeps on the earth." So God created man in His own image; in the image of God He created him; male and female He created them.
>
> —Genesis 1:26–27

Note the word *Our*. We have been created in the full image of God the Father, God the Son, and God the Holy Spirit. To be created in God's image means that He has given us His qualities: we have an ability to know things and remember them, we have an ability to feel emotions and to respond to life with a full range of feelings, and we have an ability to make choices and decisions, to solve problems, to have "dominion" or authority over creation. We also have God's ability to help, to teach, to testify, to call to remembrance, to give convincing arguments. God has created us with the full capacity to be people.

As part of our creation, God "breathed" Himself into us. We have the specific ability to know God, to sense Him at work in us, and to respond to Him. He made us with the capacity to be His children and to invite Him into our lives.

The Holy Spirit is the Spirit of God, and we are wise to refer to Him in just that way:

&. The Holy Spirit of God almighty

13

✎ The Holy Spirit of Christ Jesus—the same Spirit who indwelled Christ

✎ The Holy Spirit who indwells us today

All are one and the same Holy Spirit! His role in the Trinity is to fill, to energize, to empower, to compel behavior, to produce qualities of character, to work in and through God's creation. He is not the Creator, but there is no creation without Him. He is not the Father, but there is no confirmation of our relationship with the Father without Him. He is not the entire summation of God almighty, but there is no expression of God's will apart from Him. He is not the Son, but there is no awareness of sin and no saving knowledge of Jesus Christ apart from Him. He is not Jesus, but Jesus did not do anything apart from the Holy Spirit's empowerment.

The Holy Spirit is inseparable from Christ Jesus and from God the Father.

> But when the Helper comes, whom I shall send to you from the Father, the Spirit of truth who proceeds from the Father, He will testify of Me.
>
> —John 15:26

✎ What does this verse reveal about the triune Godhead—Father, Son, and Holy Spirit?

14

*⸱ Why is it important to understand that the Holy Spirit is part of the Trinity of God?

The Holy Spirit Is God's Promise to the Believer

The Holy Spirit has a unique relationship with believers. The Bible states that, if you have Christ, you have the Holy Spirit of God. He is the seal of your commitment to Jesus Christ. In other words, when you accept Jesus Christ as the atonement for your sins, the Holy Spirit automatically seals that decision before the Father in heaven. You belong to God forever. There is no unsealing of what the Holy Spirit seals, not by your actions or by the actions of any other person.

Conversely, if you do not have the Holy Spirit living in you, you haven't received Jesus Christ as your Savior. He is God's seal and guarantee on your life; He is proof of God's claim that you belong to Him. A person cannot be a Christian and not have the Holy Spirit within.

Some people ask, "Have you received the Holy Spirit since you became a Christian?"

This question is an impossibility. You received the Holy Spirit *as part of your receiving Christ.* You can't receive just one part of the Trinity. When you became a Christian—when you confessed your sins and asked for God's forgiveness—you received the Holy Spirit. The Spirit of God came and indwelled your spirit and claimed you as His own. He has put you into full relationship with the Father and the Son, because He is inseparable from the Father and the Son. He now works to live

His life—the same quality of life that Jesus Christ lived—in you and through you.

☙ Have you accepted Jesus Christ as your Savior? If not, what is preventing you?

☙ If you are a Christian, how do you know for sure that the Holy Spirit is within you?

The Promise to Every Believer

Jesus promised the Holy Spirit to His disciples, and that promise extends to us as His disciples today. Jesus said, "But the Helper, the Holy Spirit, whom the Father will send in My name, He will teach you all things" (John 14:26). Jesus said the Father *will* send the Spirit. At the time of Jesus' ascension, He said to His disciples, "Behold, I send the Promise of My Father upon you; but tarry in the city of Jerusalem until you are endued with power from on high" (Luke 24:49). It was the promise that Jesus had made to them on the night of the Last Supper— the promise of the Holy Spirit's coming to them to help and comfort them in His absence.

In Acts 1:8, we find these additional words at the time of Jesus' ascension: "You shall receive power *when* the Holy Spirit has come upon you; and you shall be witnesses to Me in Jerusalem, and in all Judea and Samaria, and to the end of the earth" (emphasis added). There was no doubt in His mind that it would happen for those who followed Him.

Read Peter's description of the events on the day of Pentecost:

> This Jesus God has raised up, of which we are all witnesses. Therefore being exalted to the right hand of God, and having received from the Father the promise of the Holy Spirit, He poured out this which you now see and hear.

> —Acts 2:32–33

Peter was saying, "We received the One who was promised. You witnessed the manifestation of His presence coming into our lives with your own eyes and ears." The Holy Spirit is God's promise to you as His child today. If you are a follower of the Lord Jesus Christ, you have the Holy Spirit living in you.

The Holy Spirit Is the Power of the Believer

Jesus promised the Holy Spirit to those who followed Him because He knew that they would need the Holy Spirit in them if they were to be faithful, steadfast, and effective in their walk with God. The Holy Spirit enables people to live the Christian life.

Paul wanted the believers in Ephesus to know that they had full resurrection power in their lives. They had the same power that raised Christ Jesus from the dead. Certainly, such power was able to raise them from their sins. Not only that, but the power is above any other principality, power, dominion, or might. Nothing is more powerful than the Holy Spirit in you.

> Now to Him who is able to do exceedingly abundantly above all that we ask or think, according to the power that works in us, to Him be glory in the church by Christ Jesus to all generations, forever and ever. Amen.
>
> —Ephesians 3:20–21

❧ According to these verses, what is the Holy Spirit able to do in your life?

❧ What is the "power that works in us"? What does this power accomplish?

☙ Today and Tomorrow ❧

TODAY: THE HOLY SPIRIT IS PART OF THE TRINITY OF GOD, AND HE BRINGS GOD'S POWER TO MY LIFE.

TOMORROW: I WILL SPEND TIME THIS WEEK STUDYING WHAT THE BIBLE TEACHES CONCERNING THE SPIRIT'S POWER IN MY LIFE.

☙ Notes and Prayer Requests: ❧

Lesson 3

Relying on the Holy Spirit's Power in Us

---- ✑ **In This Lesson** ✒ ----

LEARNING: WHAT DOES THE HOLY SPIRIT DO FOR A CHRISTIAN?

GROWING: HOW AM I TO RESPOND TO HIS PRESENCE IN MY LIFE?

⌾

The Holy Spirit's power in Christians is described by the Greek word *dunamis*, from which we get the English word *dynamite*. The Holy Spirit causes things to happen! His is an infinite power that blasts sin out of our lives. In this lesson, we will examine the characteristics of the Holy Spirit's power in us.

The Holy Spirit Purifies Us

First and foremost, the power of the Holy Spirit purifies us. The nature of the Holy Spirit is often identified with fire. You will recall that the Holy Spirit's manifestation is described as "divided tongues, as of fire" (Acts 2:3).

Fire or intense temperature is used to melt and purify metals. This image appears in the Old Testament applying to God's people: God will "thoroughly purge away your dross, and take away all your alloy" (Isa. 1:25). This same imagery can be applied to God's purification of all that makes you impure before the Father. The Holy Spirit burns sin out of you so that you won't burn in your sin.

Paul wrote to the Romans, "If Christ is in you, the body is dead because of sin, but the Spirit is life because of righteousness. But if the Spirit of Him who raised Jesus from the dead dwells in you, He who raised Christ from the dead will also give life to your mortal bodies through His Spirit who dwells in you" (Rom. 8:10-11). The Holy Spirit burns sin from us, and He cleanses the fleshly nature so that we no longer desire to sin. In other words, once He has purified us, part of the purification process is a desire to remain pure.

> Looking for the blessed hope and glorious appearing of our great God and Savior Jesus Christ, who gave Himself for us, that He might redeem us from every lawless deed and purify for Himself His own special people, zealous for good works.
>
> —Titus 2:13–14

What does it mean to be "zealous for good works"? Give practical examples.

How does the Holy Spirit "redeem us from every lawless deed"? Give practical examples.

Fire and burning are not comfortable images to us. Fire sounds painful, and sometimes the fire of the Holy Spirit in our lives *is* painful. His chastisement and admonishment often go against what we desire in the fleshly, human nature. But the results of His purification process are glorious! As the Lord purifies us, we are made acceptable in His sight and are made ready for use in His kingdom. Purification is a necessary part of being sanctified, which is to be cleansed and set aside as holy in God's eyes.

Purity of heart cannot be separated from the power of the Holy Spirit. That's a vital concept to understand. You are purified by the Holy Spirit, and you continue to walk in purity because of the Holy Spirit's presence and power in you. There is no way that you can clean up your life apart from His enabling you to do so.

Many people attempt to clean up their lives by a change in their behavior. They start going to church, attending a Bible study, giving some of their money to God, reading their Bibles, saying their prayers. None of these actions drives sin from their lives. Only as they yield to the Holy Spirit can they truly be cleansed completely.

⁓ How has the Holy Spirit worked in your life to refine your character?

⁓ When have you found the Holy Spirit's purifying to be painful? In what areas have you seen true change? Was the change worth the temporary discomfort?

The Role of Conviction in Purification

Before we can be cleansed of sin, we must first be convicted that we *have* sinned. That is part of the Holy Spirit's purification process in us. Paul wrote about this to the Corinthians. He asked them, "Do you not know that you are the temple of God and that the Spirit of God dwells in you? If anyone defiles the temple of God, God will destroy him. For the temple of God is holy, which temple you are" (1 Cor. 3:16-17).

No believer in Christ Jesus would think of defacing or destroying a church building. We consider our churches to be sacred places. In like manner, Paul taught the Corinthians that their bodies were sacred places. They were indwelled by God's Holy Spirit, just as the temple of old was filled with God's Holy Spirit.

In other words, the Corinthians had no right to themselves any longer. They belonged to God. They were His possessions. The Holy Spirit will not allow anything that is not holy, pure, and righteous to coexist with Him in His temple. For that reason, the Holy Spirit convicts us continually when we sin. We may turn a deaf ear to His conviction for such a long period that it seems as if His conviction has been reduced to a whisper, but He will convict us of our sin until we confess it, repent of it, and are cleansed of it. Our sin is a stain on our purity before God, and the Holy Spirit will not allow it to stand unchallenged.

Be sensitive to the convicting power of the Holy Spirit in your life. Respond to Him with a contrite and humble heart. Face your sin. Only then can you be forgiven of it and restored to the purity necessary for the Lord to use you as He desires to use you.

And when [the Holy Spirit] has come, He will convict the world of sin, and of righteousness, and of judgment.

—John 16:8

&. Why is it important for the Holy Spirit to convict us of sin? What would happen if He didn't?

&. How is the Holy Spirit necessary for us to gain righteousness?

The Holy Spirit Strengthens Us

A second aspect of the Holy Spirit's power is to impart strength to us. Paul prayed for the Ephesians that the Lord "would grant you, according to the riches of His glory, to be strengthened with might through His Spirit in the inner man" (Eph. 3:16). To be made strong implies that a person is initially weak by nature or has been weakened by circumstance. That certainly is true for any of us who are honest with ourselves. We struggle in staying obedient to God's Word. We are fragile in our bodies, frail in our resolve, and failing in our courage. We are weak creatures apart from the Holy Spirit.

Paul admonished the Ephesians that they were to grow into maturity in Christ "to the measure of the stature of the fullness of Christ; that we should no longer be children, tossed to and fro and carried about with every wind of doctrine, by the trickery of men, in the cunning craftiness of deceitful plotting" (Eph. 4:13-14). We are to *become* strong in Christ, and the only way that we can is through the Holy Spirit. Without the Holy Spirit, you are weak. With the Holy Spirit, you are strong, even to the point that you can "do all things through Christ" who strengthens you (Phil. 4:13).

The Spirit of Christ is the same Holy Spirit who is working in your life. You *can* do all things that God commands you to do. You *can* live a quality of life that is the same as that lived by Christ Jesus. You *can* live a life free of sin and bold in speech and action because you are empowered by the same Holy Spirit who empowered Jesus.

Paul encouraged the Corinthians along these lines by reciting for them a long list of troubles that he had experienced. He concluded, "Therefore most gladly I will rather boast in my infirmities, that the power of Christ may rest upon me.... For when I am weak, then I am strong" (2 Cor. 12:9–10). Paul knew the reality of the Holy Spirit's power in his life, strengthening him to withstand all kinds of persecution, dangers, weariness, and physical deprivation—including hunger, thirst, cold, and nakedness. He knew the power of the Holy Spirit strengthening him in times when he was afflicted by a "thorn in the flesh." (See 2 Cor. 11:23–12:7.) He told the Corinthians that he had learned this truth from the Lord: "My grace is sufficient for you, for My strength is made perfect in weakness" (2 Cor. 12:9). Paul was no stranger to hardship, but he was also no stranger to God's power working in him. He knew that the source of his strength was solely the Lord.

The Holy Spirit revives us and gives us strength when we are weakened by disease, injury, or natural calamity. The Holy Spirit enables us to endure pain and times of trial. The Holy Spirit enables us to say no to temptation, strengthening us in our resolve to be obedient to what God has commanded us to do. The Holy Spirit enables us to endure "to the end" in faith (Matt. 24:13).

And He said to me, "My grace is sufficient for you, for My strength is made perfect in weakness." Therefore most gladly I will rather boast in my infirmities, that the power of Christ may rest upon me.

—2 Corinthians 12:9

What does it mean to have God's strength made perfect through your weakness? When have you seen this in your own life or someone else's life?

What does it mean that God's grace is sufficient for you? When have you seen this in your own life or someone else's life?

Victory Over the Enemy

Ultimately, we are made strong by the power of the Holy Spirit so that we might defeat the devil. We are empowered against his

☙ *temptations*. The Holy Spirit helps us to resist impulses to sin against God and others (1 Cor. 10:12–13).

☙ *lies*. The Holy Spirit, as the Spirit of truth, helps us discern truth from lies and to see the ploy of the devil against us (John 16:13).

☙ *attacks*. The Holy Spirit is part of our defensive armor against the enemy's assault (Eph. 6:18).

We are strengthened to resist the devil and to defeat his influence in our lives. (See James 4:7.) The devil accuses us before the Father at every turn of the road in our lives, but God's promise is that we have the strength of the Holy Spirit to withstand any of the devil's activity against us. Thus, we make his accusations null and void. (See Rev. 12:10.) The Holy Spirit is omnipotent. He has all the power you can ever need or use—and infinitely more. Ask the Holy Spirit to impart the strength you need today.

Then I heard a loud voice saying in heaven, "Now salvation, and strength, and the kingdom of our God, and the power of His Christ have come, for the accuser of our brethren, who accused them before our God day and night, has been cast down.

—Revelation 12:10

27

✎ Who is the "accuser of our brethren"? Why is he called by this title?

✎ What role does the Holy Spirit play in facing these accusations before God's throne? What does He do in our lives to respond to these accusations?

The Holy Spirit Equips Us for Ministry

The Holy Spirit purifies us and strengthens us so that God can use us. The Holy Spirit does His work *in* us so that He can do His work *through* us. We are not indwelled by the Holy Spirit so that we can have an ecstatic experience or feel great peace in our relationship with God. The emotions may arise as we experience the presence of the Holy Spirit at work in us, but the Holy Spirit indwells us so that we might be His witnesses and do His work on this earth.

Recall the words of Acts 1:8: "You shall receive power when the Holy Spirit has come upon you; and you shall be witnesses to Me in Jerusalem, and in all Judea and Samaria, and to the end of the earth." The foremost manifestation of the Lord's presence in our lives is that we are His witnesses. Our changed lives say something to the world in which we live. We speak with our very lives the gospel of Jesus Christ. We display by our words and deeds the power of God to transform people from a state of sinfulness to a state of righteousness. We are purified and strengthened so that we might be living vessels of God's love and power made known to others.

In other lessons we will discuss in more depth the various types of equipping that the Lord does in our lives, but let it suffice at this point to recognize this profound truth of God's Word: God wants to use *you*. He has a plan and a purpose for your life. He has a role for you to fill that only you can fill. If you are to accomplish the reason for your existence, to fulfill your destiny, and to know the inner satisfaction of a mission accomplished, you must have the power of the Holy Spirit at work in you.

We cannot succeed in God's eyes without the Holy Spirit's help. We try to do so repeatedly, and each time we fall short. Anything that we try to do apart from the Holy Spirit's help and guidance is doomed to failure. It won't last because it has nothing of His eternal presence in it. On the other hand, everything that we do in the Holy Spirit cannot help being eternal, life-giving, and a blessing to us and others. In Him, we are and have all that is necessary forever. Without Him, we are and have nothing.

... partakers of His promise in Christ through the gospel, of
which I became a minister according to the gift of the grace of
God given to me by the effective working of His power.

—Ephesians 3:6–7

∂ In what ways was Paul a "minister" of God's grace to others?
In what ways can you be a minister of God's grace?

∂ What is "the effective working" of God's power? What role
does the Holy Spirit play in that? What role do you play?

His Example Is Our Challenge

We noted in an earlier lesson that the Holy Spirit functions as helper,
teacher, and guide. All that the Holy Spirit is, He makes available to us
so that we might help, teach, guide, speak words of conviction, and call
God's truth to the remembrance of others.

The Holy Spirit has all knowledge. He gives us His wisdom so that we
might make good decisions and sound judgments. The Holy Spirit has
capacity for all emotion. He imparts to us His great heart so that we

might love others with an expanded ability. The Holy Spirit operates out of His will. He imparts to us a knowledge of His will so that we might move in strength and obedience, and avoid the pitfalls of sin.

Ask the Holy Spirit today how He desires you to give testimony to His presence in your life and in what areas you need to let His witness shine brighter through you. What He calls you to do, He also equips you to do.

> Now may the God of peace Himself sanctify you completely; and may your whole spirit, soul, and body be preserved blameless at the coming of our Lord Jesus Christ. He who calls you is faithful, who also will do it.
>
> —1 Thessalonians 5:23–24

∽ What does it mean to be sanctified completely?

∽ Why does Paul include spirit, soul, and body in this promise? What does that teach about the Holy Spirit?

❧ Today and Tomorrow ☙

TODAY: THE HOLY SPIRIT GIVES ME EVERYTHING I NEED TO PURIFY MY LIFE AND CONQUER THE ENEMY.

TOMORROW: I WILL ASK THE LORD THIS WEEK TO SHOW ME AREAS IN MY LIFE WHICH NEED TO BE PURIFIED.

❧ Notes and Prayer Requests: ☙

Relying on the Holy Spirit's Presence

❧ In This Lesson ☙

Learning: Does the Holy Spirit ever abandon a Christian?

Growing: How does the Holy Spirit make me more like Jesus?

Sometimes people speak in terms of a filling of the Holy Spirit and then a refilling of the Holy Spirit in a person's life. Let me assure you of this truth based on God's Word: when the Holy Spirit indwells you, He abides with you forever. He does not come and go. He is with you, from now into eternity.

Jesus had an encounter with a Samaritan woman at the well near the town of Sychar. Jesus asked her to give Him a drink from the well. She was puzzled that a Jew would ask a Samaritan for a drink, and He replied, "If you knew the gift of God, and who it is who says to you, 'Give Me a drink,' you would have asked Him, and He would have given you living water." She questioned the nature of the living water and Jesus said, "Whoever drinks of this water will thirst again, but whoever drinks of the water that I shall give him will never thirst. But the water that I shall give him will become in him a fountain of water springing up into everlasting life." (See John 4:1–14.)

Jesus said to a multitude, "If anyone thirsts, let him come to Me and drink. He who believes in Me, as the Scripture has said, out of his heart will flow rivers of living water." John made it clear that Jesus was referring to the Holy Spirit as living water. He wrote, "But this He spoke concerning the Spirit, whom those believing in Him would receive; for the Holy Spirit was not yet given, because Jesus was not yet glorified." (See John 7:37–39.)

Living water refers to artesian springs—water that bubbles up through the earth in unending supply. The water from artesian springs is considered the purest, finest water available to mankind. It flows freely without end. This is the description that Jesus uses for the Holy Spirit: a freely flowing, unending inner source of purity, strength, power, and refreshment.

∼ In what ways does the Holy Spirit's ministry resemble "living waters"?

∼ What sorts of "thirst" does the Holy Spirit quench? When have you seen Him quench a thirst in your own life?

Not Yet Given?

John said that the Holy Spirit "was not yet given, because Jesus was not yet glorified" (John 7:39). This is further explained in John 14:15–18:

> If you love Me, keep My commandments. And I will pray the Father, and He will give you another Helper, that He may abide with you forever—the Spirit of truth, whom the world cannot receive, because it neither sees Him nor knows Him; but you know Him, for He dwells with you and will be in you. I will not leave you orphans; I will come to you.

Jesus is promising to send the very Spirit of God that indwells Him to comfort and help His disciples. He makes it plain that His disciples will recognize the Holy Spirit because they have known Him, as He has been manifested in Jesus. Furthermore, He says that the Holy Spirit will not be *with* them, which is the way that they had thus far experienced the Holy Spirit in the life of Jesus, but that the Holy Spirit will be *in* them.

Jesus then repeats His command that they keep His word and explains further, "If anyone loves Me, he will keep My word; and My Father will love him, and We will come to him and make Our home with him" (John 14:23). Again, we see that the Holy Spirit who indwelled and worked through Jesus is the same Holy Spirit who is made available to us today as followers of Jesus.

Jesus tells His disciples that the "Helper, the Holy Spirit, whom the Father will send in My name, He will teach you all things, and bring to your remembrance all things that I said to you" (John 14:26). He commands His disciples to abide in Him and to bear fruit. (See John 15:1-10.) He warns His disciples of persecution that will come and repeats His desire that they love one another.

But when the Helper comes, whom I shall send to you from the Father, the Spirit of truth who proceeds from the Father, He will testify of Me. And you also will bear witness, because you have been with Me from the beginning.

—John 15:26–27

Again, we see that the Holy Spirit comes from the Father at the request of Jesus. The Holy Spirit will testify, Jesus says, about what Jesus is about to do on the cross—in other words, about His becoming our all-sufficient atonement for sin. Jesus says that He is telling His disciples all these things so that they won't stumble. Then He says,

It is to your advantage that I go away; for if I do not go away, the Helper will not come to you; but if I depart, I will send Him to you. And when He has come, He will convict the world of sin, and of righteousness, and of judgment: of sin, because they do not believe in Me; of righteousness, because I go to My Father and you see Me no more; of judgment, because the ruler of this world is judged.... He, the Spirit of truth ... will guide you into all truth; for He will not speak on His own authority, but whatever He hears He will speak; and He will tell you things to come. He will glorify Me, for He will take of what is Mine and declare it to you.

—John 16:7–14

The disciples are puzzled about how it can be more advantageous for Jesus to be away from them than for Him to be with them. Jesus, knowing their thoughts, says,

And in that day you will ask Me nothing.... Whatever you ask the Father in My name He will give you. Until now you have

36

asked nothing in My name. Ask, and you will receive, that your
joy may be full.

—John 16:23–24

Up to now, the disciples have turned to Jesus for everything. They have
trusted the Holy Spirit to work in Jesus to meet their needs and to
deliver the people. After His death, resurrection, and ascension, the
disciples no longer will have Jesus present with them in bodily form.
But they will have the Holy Spirit inside them, they will be able to ask
the Father in Jesus' name to meet their needs, and the Holy Spirit will
work through them directly. That's why Jesus' going away is to their
advantage. They will have the unlimited Holy Spirit of Christ available
to them. Until Jesus is crucified and resurrected, however, this will not
happen. Until Jesus has gone away, He cannot send the Holy Spirit to
His disciples.

As Jesus is about to ascend to His Father, He gathers His disciples together for one last word. We read, "He commanded them not to depart
from Jerusalem, but to wait for the Promise of the Father, 'which,' He
said, 'you have heard from Me; for John truly baptized with water, but
you shall be baptized with the Holy Spirit not many days from now'"
(Acts 1:4-5).

Jesus promises that the Holy Spirit will come *after* He has been glorified (through His death, resurrection, and ascension). He says that the
Holy Spirit will be *in* His disciples. And He says that the Holy Spirit will
be in them as living water, a continually available source of divine assistance. Jesus says nothing of the Spirit departing from His disciples
at any time.

⮹ Why is it beneficial to have the Holy Spirit dwelling in you personally? Why did Jesus need to ascend to heaven for this to take place?

⮹ What does it mean that the Holy Spirit "will not speak on His own authority"? What does He speak to us?

The Holy Spirit's Presence in the Old Testament

This certainly must have been good news to the disciples, but it was also news that they had difficulty understanding. Until that time, the Holy Spirit had not come to stay in the lives of men and women. That was not the pattern in the Old Testament.

In the Old Testament, we have repeated mention of the Holy Spirit and His empowerment of people to perform certain tasks. But there is a major difference between the operation of the Holy Spirit in the Old Testament and what Jesus promised to His disciples. The Holy Spirit came to individuals in the Old Testament to help them with specific works or ministries, and then He departed from them.

Then the Lord spoke to Moses, saying: "See, I have called by name Bezalel the son of Uri, the son of Hur, of the tribe of Judah. And I have filled him with the Spirit of God, in wisdom, in understanding, in knowledge, and in all manner of workmanship, to design artistic works, to work in gold, in silver, in bronze, in cutting jewels for setting, in carving wood, and to work in all manner of workmanship."

—Exodus 31:1–5

The Lord sent His Spirit to Bezalel when the Israelites were commanded to construct the tabernacle. Why did Bezalel need the Holy Spirit?

Note that the Lord specifically sent His Spirit to Bazalel but not to others. What does this show us of the Holy Spirit's role in the Old Testament? How is it different in Christians today?

In each Old Testament instance, the Spirit of the Lord came upon certain people to help them fulfill leadership roles—to help them carry out God's plan and purpose among His people. Even so, He helped in a wide variety of ways—artisans, judges, warriors, kings.

39

In other instances in the Old Testament, the Spirit comes upon people so that they may prophesy or speak in the name of the Lord. In Isaiah 61:1, we read,

The Spirit of the Lord God is upon Me,
Because the Lord has anointed Me
To preach good tidings to the poor.

Ezekiel speaks about an indwelling of the Spirit to allow him to prophesy: "And He said to me, 'Son of man, stand on your feet, and I will speak to you.' Then the Spirit entered me when He spoke to me, and set me on my feet; and I heard Him who spoke to me" (Ezek. 2:1-2).

Now, the Holy Spirit does not work in the Old Testament in a manner contradictory to the manner in which He works in the New Testament. Certainly, the Holy Spirit works in the New Testament by providing leadership assistance and also by giving clear words of direction and truth. The difference is that the Spirit did not abide continually with the people in the Old Testament.

This is evident in the life of Saul, whom Samuel anointed to be the first king of Israel. After David was anointed king, "the Spirit of the Lord departed from Saul" (1 Sam. 16:14). The masses of people had no experience with the presence of the Holy Spirit. And we have no mention in the Old Testament of His coming to all the children of Israel at any time.

⮞ Why did the Holy Spirit come upon certain people in Old Testament times? Why did He not remain permanently?

🔖 Why was it necessary for Christ to pay the price of sin on the cross before the Holy Spirit could indwell all God's people?

The Holy Spirit in the Life of Jesus

There are several instances in the Gospels in which the Holy Spirit is at work in the lives of individuals. Elizabeth had an experience with the Holy Spirit when Mary came to her house and she heard Mary's greeting. Elizabeth's baby, John the Baptist, leaped in her womb, and Elizabeth "was filled with the Holy Spirit." She then prophesied to Mary, "Blessed are you among women, and blessed is the fruit of your womb!" (See Luke 1:41-42.)

Zacharias, Elizabeth's husband, was struck speechless for doubting that Elizabeth might conceive John the Baptist in her old age. After Zacharias declared that their baby's name was to be John, "Zacharias was filled with the Holy Spirit," and he then prophesied about the ministry that his son would have as the "prophet of the Highest." (See Luke 1:67-79.)

We read also in Luke that "there was a man in Jerusalem whose name was Simeon, and this man was just and devout, waiting for the Consolation of Israel, and the Holy Spirit was upon him. And it had been revealed to him by the Holy Spirit that he would not see death before he had seen the Lord's Christ." Furthermore, Simeon was directed to go to the temple "by the Spirit" as Jesus' parents brought Him to the temple. Simeon declared that Jesus was the long-awaited Messiah. (See Luke 2:25-32.)

Each person experienced a short-lived experience with the Holy Spirit, and the purpose appeared to be to proclaim the work of the Lord as it related ultimately to the life and ministry of Jesus. But what about the Holy Spirit in the life of Jesus Himself? We have a different picture from that of the Holy Spirit at work prior to Jesus' life.

First and foremost, Jesus was conceived by the Holy Spirit. The angel Gabriel told Mary, "The Holy Spirit will come upon you, and the power of the Highest will overshadow you; therefore, also, that Holy One who is to be born will be called the Son of God" (Luke 1:35). Every moment of Jesus' earthly existence was filled with the Holy Spirit. He was conceived by the Holy Spirit and had the Holy Spirit residing in Him continually from that moment onward.

As Mary's son, Jesus was human in every way. As God's Son, Jesus was divine in every way. In coming to earth, Jesus gave up the glory that He had as God the Son in heaven, but He did not give up His divinity.

What does it mean to be "overshadowed" by "the power of the Highest"? What does this teach you about the Holy Spirit's role in your life?

What roles did the Holy Spirit fill in each of the above New Testament examples? How does He fill those roles in your life?

❧ What Happened at Jesus' Baptism in Water? ❧

Many people erroneously conclude that Jesus received the Holy Spirit into His life at His baptism in water by John the Baptist. Read what Matthew has to say about this:

> When He had been baptized, Jesus came up immediately from the water; and behold, the heavens were opened to Him, and He saw the Spirit of God descending like a dove and alighting upon Him. And suddenly a voice came from heaven, saying, "This is My beloved Son, in whom I am well pleased."
>
> —Matthew 3:16–17

Jesus obeyed the Father in being baptized by John, and in the aftermath the Father revealed to Jesus in a special way that His earthly ministry was to begin. The manifestation by the Spirit was one of approval and of commissioning. The Spirit lighted "upon" Jesus, just as if the Father was tapping Him on the shoulder (as a king taps a knight on his shoulder with a sword). The Father declared His approval of Jesus and of the timing for His ministry to begin.

Nowhere in the Gospels do we have an account of Jesus receiving the gift of the Spirit or of His having an ecstatic or mystical experience with the Spirit. We have no mention that He grew in the Holy Spirit. We know that He "increased in wisdom and stature, and in favor with God and men" (Luke 2:52). All that refers to Jesus' growth in His humanity, not His divinity.

Jesus was fully God from His birth, even as He was fully man. He had no need to be filled with the Spirit, since He was always filled with the Spirit. He would not have been the Son of God otherwise.

↞ Why did the Holy Spirit descend "like a dove" on Jesus? What does the dove reveal about the Spirit's character?

↞ In what ways does the Holy Spirit make us more like Christ?

↞ What Happened in the Wilderness? ↠

Immediately after Jesus was baptized, the Spirit led Him into the wilderness where He was tempted by Satan. Jesus withstood the temptation completely. His human will was tested, and it emerged 100 percent in alignment with the Spirit of God. The will of Jesus and the will of the Spirit were as one.

Jesus "returned in the power of the Spirit to Galilee" after His wilderness experience. (See Luke 4:14.) This does not mean that Jesus acquired the Holy Spirit in the wilderness or that He grew in the Holy Spirit while there. Jesus, "being filled with the Holy Spirit, returned from the Jordan and was led by the Spirit into the wilderness" (Luke 4:1). Jesus was already filled to complete fullness before He entered the time of temptation.

Jesus was not diminished in any way by the encounter with the devil during those forty days and nights. The devil gave Jesus his best shots, and Jesus rebuffed every one. There was no one moment in which Jesus was operating in anything less than the full power of the Holy Spirit.

ᑫ Did Jesus Give Up the Spirit on the Cross? ᑫ

No, He gave up His earthly sinless life as a sacrifice for our sins. He died as the Son of God. We have no mention in the Scriptures that Jesus lost or gave up the Holy Spirit upon His crucifixion, at the time of His resurrection, or at the time of His ascension to the Father. He is filled with the Holy Spirit always. There has never been a moment throughout the ages when it has been otherwise. This permanent, unchanging presence of the Holy Spirit in Jesus' life qualifies Him as a member of the holy Trinity.

Jesus said repeatedly to His disciples that He didn't do anything that He didn't see the Father doing (John 5:19); He and the Father were one (John 10:30); and He knew the Father just as the Father knew Him (John 10:15). Jesus' entire ministry was marked by the fullness of the Holy Spirit.

ᑫ How does the Holy Spirit do the same things for us that He did through Christ?

ᑫ If a Christian has the same Holy Spirit within him that Jesus had, what does this suggest about our power over temptation?

The Holy Spirit and the Birth of the Church

On the day of Pentecost, Jesus sent His own Spirit, the Holy Spirit, to infill His church—His body of believers—just as His earthly physical body had once been filled. All believers in Christ are now His body:

> For as the body is one and has many members, but all the members of that one body, being many, are one body, so also is Christ. For by one Spirit we were all baptized into one body—whether Jews or Greeks, whether slaves or free—and have all been made to drink into one Spirit.
>
> —1 Corinthians 12:12–13

On the day of Pentecost (the fiftieth day after the Passover feast), the Father extended the same Holy Spirit that resided in Jesus to infill all who believed and accepted what Jesus did on the cross. He sealed their redemption in so doing. (See Eph. 1:13.) The glorious event of the Holy Spirit coming to Jesus' disciples marks the birthday of the church. It is the beginning of a new and lasting manifestation of the Holy Spirit.

The Holy Spirit in us is the life of Christ in us. It is His Spirit, in His body (ours individually and ours collectively as we are connected to other believers). And just as the Holy Spirit never departed from the life of Christ Jesus, so the Holy Spirit never departs from us. What a marvelous blessing He has made available to us—a blessing unknown by all who lived prior to the Cross!

☙ What does it mean to be a member of the body of Christ?

46

๑. What does it mean that we "have all been made to drink into one Spirit"? What does the verb "drink" suggest about the Spirit's presence in our lives?

Why Don't We Feel His Presence Always?

You may say, "If the Holy Spirit doesn't depart from me, why don't I always feel His presence?" There are many reasons. Sin limits the work of the Holy Spirit within you. The Lord may be chastising you or disciplining you in a certain way, and you may not feel the approval of the Holy Spirit until you conform to God's will for you. At times you may be too caught up in your activities and schedule to spend time with the Holy Spirit. None of these circumstances is an indication that the Spirit has departed from you. On the contrary, if there has been any "departing," it is your own doing.

Feelings rise and fall, come and go—but the Spirit does not. In other words, we may feel the Spirit in one time and place, and not in another time and place—not because of who He is in us, but because of the capricious nature of our human emotions.

And finally, the Holy Spirit grants special endowments of His presence and power at certain times. There are anointings associated with some ministry tasks and responsibilities. There are times when the Holy Spirit chooses to reveal Himself to us in powerful ways to encourage us, give us boldness, or cause us to take a specific action. This does not mean that the Holy Spirit comes and goes from us; rather, we more readily or more powerfully experience His presence and power in us at certain times.

You are sealed as Christ's own forever by the Holy Spirit the moment you confess your sins and receive the Father's forgiveness. It's up to you to abide in His presence, for He certainly is abiding in you.

> Then Peter said to them, "Repent, and let every one of you be baptized in the name of Jesus Christ for the remission of sins; and you shall receive the gift of the Holy Spirit. For the promise is to you and to your children, and to all who are afar off, as many as the Lord our God will call."
>
> —Acts 2:38–39

⁓ Why is the Holy Spirit referred to as a "gift"? What does this teach about His character? His availability?

⁓ What is required of a person to receive the Holy Spirit?

❧ Today and Tomorrow ❧

TODAY: GOD GIVES HIS SPIRIT TO ALL CHRISTIANS—PERMANENTLY.

TOMORROW: I WILL PRAISE THE FATHER FOR THE TREMENDOUS GIFT OF HIS SPIRIT IN MY LIFE.

❧ Notes and Prayer Requests: ❧

LESSON 5

Relying on the Holy Spirit in Prayer

———— ☙ **In This Lesson** ❧ ————

LEARNING: WHAT IS THE PURPOSE OF PRAYER?

GROWING: WHAT IF I DON'T KNOW HOW TO PRAY?

⌀

Do you struggle in prayer? If you do, you aren't alone. Every Christian I know struggles at times in prayer, wondering, "How should I pray for this situation or this person? What is the Father's will in this instance? How should I express myself to the Father to convey what I really mean?" At times, our emotions run too deep for words, and we are therefore at a loss for words in prayer. At other times, we are confused by what we see as conflicting possibilities or problems. At still other times, we feel under such heavy assault from the devil that we seem to be fighting for our very lives, and all we can voice is a desperate cry for help!

Have you ever stopped to recognize that Jesus, in His humanity, struggled with prayer? Jesus knew that He had come to the earth to be the all-sufficient atonement for sin. He said to His disciples during the final week of His life,

> The hour has come that the Son of Man should be glorified. Most assuredly, I say to you, unless a grain of wheat falls into the ground and dies, it remains alone; but if it dies, it produces much grain.... Now My soul is troubled, and what shall I say?

"Father, save Me from this hour"? But for this purpose I came to this hour. "Father, glorify Your name."

—John 12:23–24, 27–28

Even with this knowledge and resolve, Jesus struggled. Matthew tells us that, in the final hours before His betrayal by Judas, Jesus agonized in prayer in the Garden of Gethsemane. He admitted to His disciples, "My soul is exceedingly sorrowful, even to death. Stay here and watch with Me." Jesus prayed that, if at all possible, He might be spared His crucifixion. Yet His ultimate prayer was, "O My Father, if this cup cannot pass away from Me unless I drink it, Your will be done." (See Matt. 26:37–42.) Luke adds that Jesus was in such agony as He prayed that "His sweat became like great drops of blood falling down to the ground" (Luke 22:44).

Yes, Jesus struggled with prayer. So do we if prayer means anything at all to us and if we feel a burden to intercede for others. And yet, in those times of struggle, the apostle Paul taught, we can take heart because "The Spirit also helps in our weaknesses. For we do not know what we should pray for as we ought, but the Spirit Himself makes intercession for us with groanings which cannot be uttered" (Rom. 8:26).

The Holy Spirit dwells within us to help us in our prayer lives! We can count on Him to make our prayers effective.

☙ What does Paul mean when he says, "We do not know what we should pray for as we ought"? When have you felt that way?

✎ What "weaknesses" does the Holy Spirit help with when it comes to prayer?

As We Pray

Jesus said that He would send a Helper to us—One who would be with us, in us, and upon us. He guides our prayers in very specific ways *as we pray*—by teaching us the meaning of God's Word and the words of Jesus as they apply to our particular situation, by reminding us of God's commandments and promises, by speaking to us of what Jesus did in His lifetime and through His death, by convicting us of sin, by guiding us into the way of righteousness before the Father, and by giving us the ability to judge right from wrong.

> But when the Helper comes, whom I shall send to you from the Father, the Spirit of truth who proceeds from the Father, He will testify of Me.

> —John 15:26

✎ What does Jesus mean when He says that the Holy Spirit will "testify" of Him? What does this have to do with prayer?

∽ Why is the Holy Spirit called "the Spirit of truth"? What does this have to do with prayer?

Praying Within the Father's Will for Us

Our desire as Christians must always be to pray within the will of the Father for us. The Father's will includes all that is beneficial and good for us personally, and all that is beneficial and good for all His children—simultaneously and eternally. His plan is greater than our ability to understand it; His purposes for our lives are beyond our comprehension. How, then, do we pray within the Father's will?

If we are praying for unsaved people, our prayer should be that they come to accept Jesus Christ as their personal Savior and then to follow Him as their Lord. If we are praying for fellow believers in Christ Jesus, certain things are always within the will of the Father. We have a good model for this in Paul's letter to the Philippians, in which he tells the Philippians what he prays for them:

> I thank my God upon every remembrance of you, always in every prayer of mine making request for you all with joy, for your fellowship in the gospel from the first day until now, being confident of this very thing, that He who has begun a good work in you will complete it until the day of Jesus Christ.... And this I pray, that your love may abound still more and more in knowledge and all discernment, that you may approve the

things that are excellent, that you may be sincere and without offense till the day of Christ, being filled with the fruits of righteousness which are by Jesus Christ, to the glory and praise of God.

—Philippians 1:3–6, 9–11

We can pray these things for all believers at all times, in all situations:

᭞ That Christ will complete the work in them that He has started

᭞ That their love may abound

᭞ That they may grow in knowledge and discernment

᭞ That they may live sincere lives as they follow Christ, never bringing offense to His name

᭞ That they may be filled with the fruits of righteousness

᭞ That their lives may bring glory and praise to God

Colossians provides another model prayer that we can always pray for our fellow believers in God's will:

[We] do not cease to pray for you, and to ask that you may be filled with the knowledge of His will in all wisdom and spiritual understanding; that you may walk worthy of the Lord, fully pleasing Him, being fruitful in every good work and increasing in the knowledge of God; strengthened with all might, according to His glorious power, for all patience and longsuffering with joy; giving thanks to the Father who has qualified us to be partakers of the inheritance of the saints in the light.

—Colossians 1:9–12

It is God's will that our fellow believers know God's will, have God's wisdom, grow in spiritual understanding, walk in righteousness, bear fruit, grow in intimacy with the Lord, and be strong, patient, and joyful. I encourage you to use these prayers as your basic pattern of intercession for others.

∽ Do you thank God for the Christian friends in your life? Why might this be within God's will for your prayer life?

∽ Put the following prayer items into your own words, then pray for others this week:

Filled with knowledge of God's will:

Filled with wisdom:

Filled with spiritual understanding:

Walk worthy of the Lord:

Fruitful in every good work:

Strengthened with all might:

Grow in intimacy with the Lord:

When We Don't Know What to Pray

Our struggle to pray within the will of the Father occurs most often when we don't know how to pray. Several years ago, I visited a woman in the hospital. She was very ill, and she asked me to pray for her healing. I tried to pray as she requested, but I found myself praying for everything but healing. In my spirit, I had a growing knowledge that healing was not God's plan for her. He was about to call her home. Sure enough, she died the next day.

In the difficult times when we don't know how to pray, or we find ourselves stopped from praying what we had intended to pray, Paul tells us that the Holy Spirit "helps in our weaknesses" (Rom. 8:26). This phrase in Greek literally means that the Holy Spirit shares the load. He gets up under the burden that we feel about our lives or others' lives, and He helps carry the prayer.

This same Greek word for help is used in Luke 10 where we read that Martha was distracted from sitting at Jesus' feet because she was concerned about getting a meal on the table. She asked Jesus to tell her sister to help her in the serving preparations. (See Luke 10:40.)

The implication in both places is that the help is practical in nature. Martha is "cumbered about" (as the King James Version says) with serving her guests. This phrase implies that she was running in circles. That's the way we often feel in our prayers, isn't it? We run all around the problem, hoping to corral it. We can trust the Holy Spirit to help us in a practical way—to guide us very specifically into God's answers and solutions so that we are praying in the will of the Father.

> The Spirit also helps in our weaknesses. For we do not know what we should pray for as we ought, but the Spirit Himself makes intercession for us with groanings which cannot be uttered."
>
> —Romans 8:26

☙ What does it mean that the Holy Spirit "makes intercession for us"?

☙ Why does He intercede "with groanings which cannot be uttered"? How is that comforting when you don't know what to pray?

What Must We Do to Receive the Holy Spirit's Help?

We need to ask for it. Ask for His help before you pray. Ask for His help as you pray. Don't allow yourself to become discouraged. When you are most discouraged about prayer, don't give in—that's the very time when you need to pray! Jesus promised that our Helper is always available and is instantly accessible. He is never out of the office when we need Him.

God values our prayers. Furthermore, He commands us to pray. Prayer is part of God's plan for accomplishing His purposes on this earth. We didn't design this plan for prayer, God did—and He wants us to succeed in prayer. That's why He helps us in it.

The Holy Spirit Understands

The Holy Spirit understands everything you think, feel, or experience. Paul says that the Spirit searches our hearts and knows the mind of the Father (Rom. 8:27). He sees with absolute clarity what we need and what the Father desires to give. The Holy Spirit understands three things simultaneously:

1. The situation that we are facing. He sees its origins. He knows all the facets and all the details.

2. Our needs within the situation. Paul wrote: "What then shall we say to these things? If God is for us, who can be against us? He who did not spare His own Son, but delivered Him up for us all, how shall He not with Him also freely give us all things?" (Rom. 8:31–32). We have everything that we need to do everything that He has called us to do.

3. The plan of God. First Corinthians 2:9–10 tells us,

"Eye has not seen, nor ear heard, nor have entered into the heart of man the things which God has prepared for those who love Him." But God has revealed them to us through His Spirit. For the Spirit searches all things, yes, the deep things of God.

As we pray, the Holy Spirit reveals the plan of God to us. We pray for everything that we can think of, and then we pause and listen for God to speak to us. We very likely won't hear Him speak with an audible voice, but suddenly we think of additional things to pray about. We pray for these things, and then we listen again. We continue this process, and we begin to receive knowledge from the Holy Spirit. We have a sense of resolution, of peace. We have deep assurance that God is answering us and that He is in control. At times, we may have clear direction—we know what to do, when to take action, and how to pursue God's answer.

We must receive this knowledge by faith and thank the Lord for it, expressing our gratitude and our intention to act on what the Lord has revealed to us. If we have misunderstood what the Lord has said to us, we can rest assured that He will be quick to correct us if we remain open to the leading and guiding of His Spirit.

Paul taught the Corinthians: "Now we have received, not the spirit of the world, but the Spirit who is from God, that we might know the things that have been freely given to us by God" (1 Cor. 2:12). As we pray, we may also find that certain ideas or words come to our minds. They may be words of Scripture or of comfort, or a message that has meaning to our specific situation. These things eventually form a pattern that is meaningful to us and represents God's answer to our need.

∾ What is "the spirit of the world"? How is it different from the Holy Spirit?

∾ What things "have been freely given to us by God"? How do these gifts affect your prayer life?

Groanings of Intercession

Paul said that the Holy Spirit "makes intercession for us with groanings which cannot be uttered" (Rom. 8:26). The Holy Spirit does not carry our *words* of prayer to Jesus Christ, who in turn presents our petitions to the Father on the basis of His shed blood. Rather, the Holy Spirit carries the *meaning* of prayer to the Father. The Holy Spirit deals with us at the deepest levels of our being, and He knows what we truly need and desire. Regardless of what we may say with our lips, the Spirit knows what we mean in our hearts. He intercedes for us at that level, which is deeper than words.

The Holy Spirit then reveals to us the Father's response in ways that we understand, although we may not be able to express that response in words. We may know, deep within, that things are going to be all right, that an answer is on its way, that we can rest assured that the prayer has been heard and God is responding with compassion and love. This means that we can never pray for the wrong thing. The Holy Spirit sees beyond our superficial understanding to the real issue that needs resolving. His answer to us is on the basis of our need and on God's plan. Therefore, His prayer for us and His answer to us are always in keeping with the will of the Father for us.

Intercessory Prayer for Others

Sometimes, we feel impressed to pray for people who are far away from us or for people that we do not know. At other times, we can't seem to get a person's name off our minds, and we feel compelled to pray on the person's behalf.

If the Father knows all that is needed, and He knows His plan, what is the purpose in praying? The Father certainly can act without our prayers. The fact is, He hasn't chosen to do so. He invites our prayers, and He uses our prayers. When we intercede for others, our faith is built up in the process. We see how God has answered, and we grow in our confidence that God sees and cares about every detail of our lives. There is a great reward in cooperating with the Holy Spirit in prayer. That reward is manifested in the lives of those for whom you pray as well as in your life.

But you, beloved, building yourselves up on your most holy faith, praying in the Holy Spirit, keep yourselves in the love of God, looking for the mercy of our Lord Jesus Christ unto eternal life.

—Jude 1:20–21

☙ What does it mean to be "building yourselves up on your most holy faith"? How is this done?

☙ In light of all that we have considered in this lesson, what does it mean to be "praying in the Holy Spirit"?

☙ What does it mean to "keep yourselves in the love of God"?

❧ Today and Tomorrow ❧

TODAY: THE HOLY SPIRIT KEEPS US IN CONSTANT CONTACT, THROUGH PRAYER, WITH THE FATHER.

TOMORROW: I WILL SPEND EXTRA TIME IN PRAYER THIS WEEK TO UNDERSTAND THE FATHER'S WILL.

❧ Notes and Prayer Requests: ❧

Avoiding Sin Against the Holy Spirit

❧ In This Lesson ❧

LEARNING: HOW IS SIN AGAINST THE HOLY SPIRIT DIFFERENT FROM OTHER SIN?

GROWING: WHAT IF I'VE COMMITTED THE UNPARDONABLE SIN?

Have you ever sinned against the Holy Spirit? Most people assume, and correctly so, that it is possible to sin against God the Father and against Jesus Christ, His Son. It is equally correct to assume that we can sin against the Holy Spirit. In fact, all sins are against the Trinity. We sin against God.

The New Testament describes three specific ways, however, in which our actions are directly against the Holy Spirit: (1) quenching the Holy Spirit, (2) grieving the Holy Spirit, and (3) blaspheming against the Holy Spirit. When we do these things, we short-circuit His power in our lives. In this lesson, we will take a look at each of these sins against the Holy Spirit and how we can avoid them in our Christian walk.

Quenching the Holy Spirit

Paul states very directly, "Do not quench the Spirit" (1 Thess. 5:19). As we discussed in an earlier lesson, fire has long been associated with the Holy Spirit. On the day of Pentecost, one of the manifestations of the Spirit was the appearance of "divided tongues, as of fire" resting on each person present. (See Acts 2:3.) Fire, in turn, is associated with cleansing, light, warmth, energy, refinement, and purifying. Appropriately, the word *quench* means "to stifle or put out." Paul is saying, "Don't put out the fire of the Holy Spirit in your life. Don't throw cold water on the fire of God in your heart."

We can never throw enough cold water on the fire of God to put out His fire completely in our lives. We cannot banish the Holy Spirit from our lives once we have confessed Christ. He has indwelled us and sealed our redemption. But we can impede the effectiveness of the Holy Spirit working in our lives. We can override His will, reject His promptings, or ignore His presence with us.

Have you ever been in the room with another person who ignored you completely? We say that such a person gave you the cold shoulder. We can do that to the Holy Spirit in our lives, and in so doing, we cut short the work that the Holy Spirit might otherwise do in us. He will not move beyond our will or beyond our invitation to work in us. His work in our lives is only as powerful and effective as we allow it to be. God's desire for us is that we be strong in the Holy Spirit—that we accept His full work in our lives and that we act boldly in the fullness of His power.

Praying always with all prayer and supplication in the Spirit, being watchful to this end with all perseverance and supplication for all the saints.

—Ephesians 6:18

∞ What is the difference between prayer and supplication? Give practical examples of each.

∞ In what way is perseverance needed in prayer?

∞ How Do We Quench the Spirit? ∞

The foremost ways that we quench the work of the Holy Spirit are:

We say no to something that God directs us to do. We choose our will over His will. We choose to go our own way. The Holy Spirit can do nothing to help us and to keep us in the center of God's plan and purpose for our lives if we willfully turn away from His leading and choose to pursue our own desires. He will not help us do something that He knows is contrary to God's best for us.

We can ignore His presence. Again, this is a matter of the will. We can go about living our lives and refuse to acknowledge His help, invite His help, or accept His help.

We can sin repeatedly. Our sin causes the Holy Spirit to abandon any positive implementation for our blessing so that He might convict us of our sin. When we sin, we evoke the chastisement of the Holy Spirit in our lives. He cannot reward our unfaithfulness. He cannot participate in our rebellion. We quench His eager desire to produce good fruit in us.

❧ What Can We Do? ☙

We can choose to keep our relationship kindled with the Spirit. Anyone who has ever camped or had a fireplace knows that it's easier to keep a fire burning than it is to build one. Maintain your ongoing relationship with the Holy Spirit. Talk to Him daily, just as you might pray to God the Father. Recognize His presence. Ask for His help. Invite Him to lead and guide you into right paths and right decisions.

When you sin, be quick to respond to His convicting nudges in your life. Confess your sin immediately, and repent of it, turning back to the way that you know God wants you to walk. When the Holy Spirit prompts you to move in a certain direction, say yes. Don't hesitate. Respond quickly to say what He compels you to say or do what He leads you to do. Choose to stay strong in the Lord.

Be strong in the Lord and in the power of His might.

—Ephesians 6:10

❧ Give practical examples of what it means to "be strong in the Lord and in the power of His might".

❧ How can these practical steps help you to avoid sinning against the Holy Spirit?

Grieving the Holy Spirit

A second way in which we short-circuit the work of the Holy Spirit is through grieving Him. Paul wrote, "Do not grieve the Holy Spirit of God, by whom you were sealed for the day of redemption" (Eph. 4:30). This admonition is embedded within a passage in which Paul admonished the believers in Ephesus to "no longer walk as the rest of the Gentiles walk" but to "put on the new man which was created according to God, in true righteousness and holiness" (Eph. 4:17, 24). He told them to put away from their lives lying (v. 25), anger (v. 26), stealing (v. 28), and corrupt speech (v. 29). He summed up his statement to them: "Let all bitterness, wrath, anger, clamor, and evil speaking be put away from you, with all malice. And be kind to one another, tenderhearted, forgiving one another, even as God in Christ forgave you" (vv. 31-32).

We grieve the Holy Spirit when we disobey God's commandments and when we choose to act in unrighteous ways. In other words, we know what to do and then choose to do the opposite. The Ephesians knew that it was not godly to lie, steal, be angry with one another, or speak cutting words to one another. They knew that such things gave "place to the devil" (v. 27).

Paul lived and ministered among the Ephesians for two years, and his ministry had a powerful impact on the city of Ephesus—and yet he had to remind the Christians not to do those things! It was as if he had to go back to square one with them. When the Ephesians broke the most obvious of God's commandments, they caused sorrow in the Holy Spirit. Paul said, "Your behavior breaks the heart of God."

The Holy Spirit is grieved because He loves us and He deeply desires to reward us, bless us, and see good fruit produced in us. He knows that sin destroys us and causes negative consequences in our lives. When we know that loved ones are doing something that will cause them harm, we are grieved. So is He.

How Can We Avoid Grieving the Holy Spirit?

We can choose to keep God's commandments and to lead a disciplined life. When we sin, we must confess the sin immediately and repent of it, changing our minds and our behavior to conform to God's statutes. As we ask the Holy Spirit to lead us and help us on a daily basis, we have His help in our Christian walk. He keeps our footing sure. He gives us the courage to withstand temptation.

> And do not grieve the Holy Spirit of God, by whom you were sealed for the day of redemption. Let all bitterness, wrath, anger, clamor, and evil speaking be put away from you, with all malice. And be kind to one another, tenderhearted, forgiving one another, even as God in Christ forgave you.
>
> —Ephesians 4:30–32

Define each of the following in your own words, with examples:

Bitterness:

Wrath:

Anger:

Clamor:

☜ Define each of the following in your own words, with examples:

Be kind:

Tenderhearted:

Forgiving:

Blaspheming Against the Holy Spirit

In Matthew 12, we read about a confrontation between Jesus and the Pharisees, some of the religious leaders who were plotting to destroy Him because of the miracles that He had done on the Sabbath. Jesus knew what the Pharisees were up to, and what their real motivations were, but He continued His work among the people and healed a man who was demon-possessed and could not see or hear. There was no doubt that the man had been healed and delivered in a powerful way.

The Pharisees were intent on destroying the credibility of Jesus, and they insisted that He had healed by the power of Beelzebub, the ruler of the demons. Jesus replied, "Every kingdom divided against itself is brought to desolation" (Matt. 12:25). In other words, Satan isn't going to empower or inspire anybody to do something that is good. Satan would be setting up his own downfall.

70

The Pharisees were also making a statement about God—that God would not empower someone like Jesus to do good on the Sabbath. They were saying that God is content to let people starve or suffer on the Sabbath, to allow people to remain demon-possessed, unable to see or hear. But the ruler of the demons, Beelzebub, is willing to see such people helped and healed. They had completely turned upside down the truth about God and the devil.

Jesus said to them, "He who is not with Me is against Me, and he who does not gather with Me scatters abroad" (Matt. 12:30). And then He added:

> Therefore I say to you, every sin and blasphemy will be for-given men, but the blasphemy against the Spirit will not be forgiven men. Anyone who speaks a word against the Son of Man, it will be forgiven him; but whoever speaks against the Holy Spirit, it will not be forgiven him, either in this age or in the age to come.
>
> —Matthew 12:31–32

Jesus was saying, "You can say what you will about Me, but don't speak such perversion about the Spirit of God. When you blaspheme against God in that way, you are saying that God does not desire to forgive and deliver people. And as long as you believe that and teach that to others, you won't be able to experience His forgiveness and deliverance. If you don't believe that God wants to forgive people and restore people to wholeness, you will never be open to the sacrifice that I will make on the cross of Calvary."

Those words of Jesus were to the Pharisees, people who had put them-selves into sharp conflict with Him and who were plotting His destruc-tion. Those words were spoken to them before the death of Jesus on the cross and before His resurrection. Those words were spoken as a warning to the Pharisees to let them know that He knew the full intent of their hearts and the full meaning of their claims. This sin of blaspheming against the Holy Spirit is called an unpardonable sin in this passage.

First, let me assure you that if you have any concern about having committed the unpardonable sin, there is no way that you have committed it. Second, this is the only time that we find these words in the Scriptures and the message is solely to the Pharisees who were cutting themselves off from the possibility of acknowledging Jesus as their Savior and Lord. At no other time in the New Testament, however, do we find mention of an unpardonable sin. There are no warnings against it or teachings about it. To the contrary, numerous passages of Scripture announce that God's forgiveness is freely given and readily available for the asking.

> If we say that we have no sin, we deceive ourselves, and the truth is not in us. If we confess our sins, He is faithful and just to forgive us our sins and to cleanse us from all unrighteousness.
>
> —1 John 1:8–9

How do these verses prove that you cannot commit a sin which God isn't willing to forgive? How does the simple act of acknowledging your sin make you eligible for forgiveness?

∽ On what basis does God forgive sins? Is there anything, besides confessing, that you must do?

We should not concern ourselves with the question of whether it is unpardonable to blaspheme against the Holy Spirit. We should focus on the more important issue: When we refuse to receive the forgiveness that God freely offers, we put ourselves into an unpardonable state. We can die in an unpardonable state, but it won't be because we have committed an unpardonable sin.

No sin is unforgivable on this side of death. It is equally true that no sin can be forgiven on the other side of the grave. Refusing to believe in the forgiveness made available to us by the death of Christ brings about everlasting death. Accepting what Jesus did on the cross—believing in Him as Savior—brings about everlasting life.

In like manner, when we willfully turn away from God and pursue the lusts of the flesh, we tie the hands of the Holy Spirit in our lives. He will not force us to experience God's will for us. He will convict us of our sin, speak to us of Jesus, and chastise us for our rebellion, but He will not override our choices.

Because you are a Christian, your rebellion will not put you into an unpardonable state, but it will put you into a miserable state! You cannot be happy or know the fullness of God's joy, peace, and blessings if you are in sin and refuse God's forgiveness. You will be cut off from the fullness of your potential and the maximum blessing that God has for you in achieving your destiny in Him. And you will remain in that miserable state until you confess your sins to God and receive His forgiveness.

For the wages of sin is death, but the gift of God is eternal life
in Christ Jesus our Lord.

—Romans 6:23

What does Paul mean when he says that the wages of sin is
death? How are wages different from gifts?

What is required of a person to receive eternal life, according
to this verse? What is the one thing that can prevent a person
from receiving that gift?

Today and Tomorrow

TODAY: MY SINFUL BEHAVIOR CAN GRIEVE AND QUENCH THE HOLY SPIR-
IT.

TOMORROW: I WILL ASK THE LORD TO SHOW ME AREAS IN MY LIFE THAT
NEED TO BE MORE HOLY.

LESSON 7

Reproducing Christ's Character in Us

---------- ⮞ **In This Lesson** ⮜ ----------

LEARNING: WHAT IS MEANT BY THE FRUIT OF THE SPIRIT?

GROWING: HOW IS THE FRUIT OF THE SPIRIT OBTAINED?

---------- ⟨❂⟩ ----------

How can you identify a Christian? The Bible's answer is that a Christian will bear the fruit of the Holy Spirit—a Christian will display the same character qualities that Jesus Christ displayed during His life on this earth. Fruit is the outward expression that we are true followers of Jesus Christ. The theme of fruit-bearing is important in the ministry of Jesus. In the Sermon on the Mount, Jesus said:

> Beware of false prophets, who come to you in sheep's clothing, but inwardly they are ravenous wolves. You will know them by their fruits. Do men gather grapes from thornbushes or figs from thistles? Even so, every good tree bears good fruit, but a bad tree bears bad fruit. A good tree cannot bear bad fruit, nor can a bad tree bear good fruit. Every tree that does not bear good fruit is cut down and thrown into the fire. Therefore by their fruits you will know them.
>
> —Matthew 7:15–20

Jesus repeated this teaching in positive terms to His disciples:

I am the true vine, and My Father is the vinedresser. Every branch in Me that does not bear fruit He takes away; and every branch that bears fruit He prunes, that it may bear more fruit.... Abide in Me, and I in you. As the branch cannot bear fruit of itself, unless it abides in the vine, neither can you, unless you abide in Me. I am the vine, you are the branches. He who abides in Me, and I in him, bears much fruit; for without Me you can do nothing. If anyone does not abide in Me, he is cast out as a branch and is withered; and they gather them and throw them into the fire, and they are burned. If you abide in Me, and My words abide in you, you will ask what you desire, and it shall be done for you. By this My Father is glorified, that you bear much fruit; so you will be My disciples.

—John 15:1–2, 4–8

Without a doubt, Jesus expects us to bear fruit in our lives—the fruit of His likeness.

✍ Why does a gardener prune a branch that already bears fruit? What does this accomplish?

✍ What does pruning involve? How might this feel to the vine? What might it involve in a person's life?

76

Peter Was a Fruit-Bearer

Peter is a great example of the Holy Spirit's working in a person's life to bear fruit. Peter had followed Jesus closely for nearly three years. He had been a witness to His many miracles. He had heard His sermons. He had watched His life. Peter had even walked on water with Jesus! But in the aftermath of Jesus' arrest in the Garden of Gethsemane, Peter denied three times that he knew his beloved Master.

But after Peter received the Holy Spirit on the day of Pentecost, he preached one of the most powerful sermons in the Scriptures and said to the very ones to whom he hadn't previously dared to open his mouth:

> Men of Israel, hear these words: Jesus of Nazareth, a Man attested by God to you by miracles, wonders, and signs which God did through Him in your midst, as you yourselves also know—Him, being delivered by the determined purpose and foreknowledge of God, you have taken by lawless hands, have crucified, and put to death
>
> —Acts 2:22–23

Those are not the words of a timid man. Those are words of bold proclamation. Peter was bearing good fruit!

Two Types of Fruit

Two types of fruit are indicated in the teachings of Scripture. The first is the fruit of works and deeds. Jesus cites this type of fruit in Matthew 7, where the false prophets are known by their evil words and deeds. The second type of fruit is of character. This inner fruit is the more

77

important since what we do is always a natural overflow of who we are. We may be able to hide our bad character behind good deeds for a while, but eventually our true character will display itself.

Galatians 5:19-23 describes the character traits that the Lord wants us to have:

> Now the works of the flesh are evident, which are: adultery, fornication, uncleanness, lewdness, idolatry, sorcery, hatred, contentions, jealousies, outbursts of wrath, selfish ambitions, dissensions, heresies, envy, murders, drunkenness, revelries, and the like; of which I tell you beforehand, just as I also told you in time past, that those who practice such things will not inherit the kingdom of God. But the fruit of the Spirit is love, joy, peace, longsuffering, kindness, goodness, faithfulness, gentleness, self-control. Against such there is no law.

God's standard for fruit bearing is righteousness, purity, and obedience to God's moral law. Paul repeatedly warned the gentile Christians that there is no provision whatsoever in the gospel for impurity. There is no license to sin.

≈ Define the following fruit in your own words, giving examples of each:

Love:

Joy:

Peace:

Longsuffering:

Kindness:

Goodness:

Faithfulness:

Gentleness:

Self-control:

The Nature of Fruit Bearing

I want you to note some aspects of fruit-bearing in the Scriptures.

First, we are commanded to bear fruit. This is not an option. The words of Jesus and the writers of the New Testament are commands. *Abide* in Me. *Bear* fruit. *Walk* in the Spirit. *Make* the tree good.

Second, we are to bear good fruit. We have a choice in the type of fruit that we will produce, and both Jesus and Paul admonish us to bear fruit that is recognized as good by God, saint, and sinner alike.

Good fruit is beautiful to behold—it is almost irresistible. Good fruit is also sound; it isn't damaged by disease or bruising. Good fruit bears within it healthy seeds that produce new life. In spiritual terms, good fruit draws others to Christ and is not tainted by sin. Such fruit has within it something that will last forever. Only the work of the Holy Spirit is truly good, for only His work is eternal and completely without blemish, compelling others to accept Christ Jesus as their Savior.

Fruit that is produced by the Holy Spirit has the same quality of goodness that is found in the Spirit Himself. In Jesus' analogy of the vine, the Holy Spirit is the life force flowing through the vine and producing fruit within us. Jesus was indwelled by the same Holy Spirit who now indwells us, and we produce the same good fruit in our lives that was manifested in Jesus' life.

The Holy Spirit is the source of any goodness in us. We may think that we are good people, but we are not good—apart from the Holy Spirit and the life of Christ that He is producing in us. Our pride causes us to think that we can produce goodness on our own.

Third, we are to bear much fruit. Our lives are to be overflowing with the fruit of the Spirit. Our character is to be overflowing with the goodness of Christ Jesus. Our love is to be abundant, our joy is to be exuberant, our peace is to be all-encompassing, and so forth. We are to be continually at work in God's kingdom, doing whatever the Lord leads us to do to the best of our ability and with the maximum effort.

The fruit mentioned in Galatians 5:22 is singular—the "fruit" of the Spirit, not the "fruits" of the Spirit. When we receive the life of the Holy

Spirit within us, we get all of the Holy Spirit. Thus, all of His traits become our traits. He doesn't award them to us bit by bit. We receive the full nature of the Holy Spirit. The abundance of fruit that we manifest, however, is subject to the will. We can refuse to do what the Spirit prompts us to do.

> I say then: Walk in the Spirit, and you shall not fulfill the lust of the flesh. For the flesh lusts against the Spirit, and the Spirit against the flesh; and these are contrary to one another, so that you do not do the things that you wish.

> —Galatians 5:16–17

How does the flesh lust against the Spirit? How does the Spirit lust against the flesh?

What does it mean to walk in the Spirit, in practical terms?

What About the Unfruitful?

Jesus said that every branch that doesn't produce is taken away or, as some translations say, "cast away" (John 15:2). There are two possible interpretations for this phrase "cast away." One is to be lifted up off the ground. In the Middle East, the branches of vines are often left to grow close to the ground rather than trained on wires or trellises as they are in Europe and the United States. To "cast away" or "take away" a branch can mean to lift up the branch to train it along a stake or wire. To "cast away" can also mean to cut off and discard. In either case, the vine is moved or removed from its current position.

In the lives of unbelievers, these words should hold a stinging conviction. Those who don't abide in Christ are subject either to being lifted up (which can mean that they confess Christ and are saved and made fruitful) or to being removed by death. If they don't abide in Christ, they are subject to change—either positive or negative.

Some people try to act as if they are producing fruit. They go through the motions of attending church, doing church work, claiming to pray and read God's Word. They'll do their best to convince you that they are people of good character. But they aren't connected to the Vine. They have never been born again and, as a result, they do not receive the life-giving, fruit-bearing sustenance of the Holy Spirit. They have not been grafted into Christ. Eventually, their state is revealed. The branches wither and are cast away.

If you have any doubt about whether you are grafted into Christ Jesus, confess to God that you are a sinner, and ask for His forgiveness today. Receive what He freely offers to give you. Then repent of your old ways and rely on the Holy Spirit to produce genuine fruit in your life.

If you are a believer and you are not producing much good fruit in your life, the Lord is not going to remove you from Himself. But He is going to continue to convict you of any sin in your life until you let it go, ask for forgiveness, and invite the Lord to cast your sin away from you. The Lord also says that those who are bearing fruit are subject to being pruned so that they will bear more fruit.

Sin can stop the flow of the Spirit in our lives and result in dead wood in our souls. Neglecting the things of God can cause dead wood. We can become so busy, and have our priorities so out of line, that the flow of the Spirit is thwarted and part of us seems to die out. If any of these conditions applies to you today, confess that to the Lord, repent of your behavior, receive His forgiveness, and make a new start in your life. Choose to bear much fruit. Invite the pruning work of the Holy Spirit into your life. Ask Him to show you in which areas you need to change your mind and your behavior.

> But fornication and all uncleanness or covetousness, let it not even be named among you, as is fitting for saints; neither filthiness, nor foolish talking, nor coarse jesting, which are not fitting, but rather giving of thanks. For this you know, that no fornicator, unclean person, nor covetous man, who is an idolater, has any inheritance in the kingdom of Christ and God.
>
> —Ephesians 5:3–5

Define each of the following in your own words, with examples:

Fornication:

Covetousness:

Filthiness:

Foolish talking:

Coarse jesting:

The Pruning Process

Pruning can be painful. It can seem drastic at times. Early in my ministry, I pastored a church in Fruitland, North Carolina. One day I called on a member of our congregation who was in his apple orchard, pruning an apple tree. I was shocked at how severely he was pruning the tree, and I said to him, "You're going to *kill* that tree." He looked at me with the eyes of many years of experience and said, "You stick to preaching and I'll do the pruning." At times, you may feel as if God is killing you with the severity of His pruning, but be encouraged. He is getting ready for a great harvest of fruit in your life.

> My brethren, count it all joy when you fall into various trials, knowing that the testing of your faith produces patience. But let patience have its perfect work, that you may be perfect and complete, lacking nothing.
>
> —James 1:2–4

◈ In what ways can "the testing of your faith" produce patience?

☞ When you find yourself in the middle of a trial, what is your initial response? What is required to "count it all joy"?

Fruit-bearing was never intended to be difficult. A cluster of grapes doesn't have to work at becoming sweet or ripe, and neither do we. The fruit-bearing in our lives is automatic if we remain in the Vine. Our job is to abide; His job is to produce fruit in us. As long as we stay true to the Lord, walk in obedience to Him, and allow Him to have control over our lives, the fruit in us grows naturally and according to His time schedule.

We can't force fruit to grow. We can only cling to Jesus and choose to follow the daily leading of the Holy Spirit in our lives. *Our heavenly Father* is the Vinedresser. *Jesus* is the Vine. The *Holy Spirit* is the life-giving force flowing through the Vine. We are the branches that bear His fruit.

> By this we know that we love the children of God, when we love God and keep His commandments. For this is the love of God, that we keep His commandments. And His commandments are not burdensome.
>
> —1 John 5:2–3

☞ What commandments might the Holy Spirit be calling you to keep more carefully? What will you do differently this week?

Why does John link love of "the children of God" with love of God Himself? How does this relate to the two greatest commandments? (See Matthew 22:38–40.)

Today and Tomorrow

TODAY: THE HOLY SPIRIT BRINGS THE FULL CHARACTER OF GOD INTO MY LIFE.

TOMORROW: I WILL PRAYERFULLY WORK ON INCREASING THE FRUIT OF THE SPIRIT THIS WEEK.

Relying on the Spirit for Spiritual Gifts

────── ☙ **In This Lesson** ❧ ──────

LEARNING: WHAT'S THE DIFFERENCE BETWEEN SPIRITUAL GIFTS AND NATU-
RAL TALENTS?

GROWING: WHAT ARE MY SPIRITUAL GIFTS?

────── ⬯ ──────

Do you feel inadequate in your ability to serve others? Do you feel in-
capable of ministry? Do you wish that your ministry to others might
be more effective? I have good news for you today! You are not alone
in your ministry. The Holy Spirit will equip you for ministry and then
help you do it. The results are completely in His hands, and what the
Holy Spirit does is always successful and effective. Paul wrote, "He who
calls you is faithful, who also will do it" (1 Thess. 5:24).

"But," you may say, "I'm not sure that now is the right time for me to
be part of a ministry to others or to take on any service to others." Now
is always the time in God's eyes. If you refuse to give yourself to others,
you will miss the blessing that comes from giving on earth and you will
miss a blessing in heaven. Of equal importance, you will be a hindrance
to the work of God. The Lord is counting on you to minister to others,
which means to serve others, give to others, help others. That's part of
the life in Christ that He has ordained for you.

Many people think of ministry only in terms of full-time church work or work as a missionary or in a church-related organization. Ministry occurs any time we do something in the name of Jesus for the benefit of others. Jesus was very clear on this point:

> "I was hungry and you gave Me food; I was thirsty and you gave Me drink; I was a stranger and you took Me in; I was naked and you clothed Me; I was sick and you visited Me; I was in prison and you came to Me." Then the righteous will answer Him, saying, "Lord, when did we see You hungry and feed You, or thirsty and give You drink? When did we see You a stranger and take You in, or naked and clothe You? Or when did we see You sick, or in prison, and come to You?" And the King will answer and say to them, "Assuredly, I say to you, inasmuch as you did it to one of the least of these My brethren, you did it to Me."
>
> —Matthew 25:35–40

The Lord expects us to be His ministers on earth—to be His hands and feet. He describes those who follow Him as His body. We are to do collectively what Jesus did in His earthly body: minister to others in healing, deliverance, and preaching good news. And because we are many in number, our ministry multiplies what Jesus did. We are to be like Him in character, in thought, in word, and in deed.

☙ When have you given hospitality to strangers or clothed the poor or fed the hungry? When has someone served you in that way?

⎷. In what ways are we actually serving Jesus when we do such things for people?

Our ministry is so important to God the Father that He sent the Holy Spirit upon Jesus' request to fill us and to enable us to minister. We minister according to the degree that we allow the Holy Spirit to work in us. Our ministry is the ministry of the Holy Spirit. We speak the words, but they are His words. We take the actions, but they are His works that He commands us to do. We are the flesh and bones, the personality and talents; He is the motivation and the life.

Think for a moment about a doctor who ministers to a patient. He does his part, prescribing the best treatment and medicine that he knows. He performs surgery if that is required, or sets broken bones or stitches wounds. But only God can heal a sick or injured body. Only God can cause life to overtake disease and death and cause a sick person to become whole again. The same goes for our work in ministering to others. We do all that we can under the direction of the Holy Spirit, but the results of that ministry are His results and His alone. He causes ministry to take root and become a living testimony in our lives.

The Spirit of the Lord God is upon Me, Because the Lord has anointed Me To preach good tidings to the poor; He has sent Me to heal the brokenhearted, To proclaim liberty to the captives, And the opening of the prison to those who are bound; To proclaim the acceptable year of the Lord, And the day of vengeance of our God; To comfort all who mourn, To console those who mourn in Zion, To give them beauty for ashes, The oil of joy for mourning, The garment of praise for the spirit of heaviness; That they may be called trees of righteousness, The planting of the LORD, that He may be glorified.

—Isaiah 61:1–3

How do you give someone beauty for ashes? Oil of joy for mourning? Garment of praise for a spirit of heaviness?

When has someone done these things in your life?

The Giver of Gifts

The Holy Spirit is a giver of many gifts to help us in our ministry. Another way to think of gifts is as enablements or helps. The Holy Spirit is described by Jesus as our Helper. He gives us what we need in the form of spiritual gifts to help us accomplish what He asks us to do.

Spiritual gifts are different from our natural gifts and talents—the abilities with which we were born. Natural abilities and talents are gifts of God, but these gifts are given to us in our humanity. They are not divine or spiritual gifts, and they never become spiritual gifts. We err if we believe that our natural gifts automatically become spiritual gifts

90

when we accept Christ Jesus. They do not. Our natural gifts remain after we accept Christ, and they are enhanced or blessed in wonderful ways because of our relationship with Christ Jesus, but they remain as natural, human gifts.

We need to explore, develop, and perfect our natural gifts. God has given them to us to use for His kingdom. We should never downplay our abilities; rather, we should develop them to their full potential. The Holy Spirit adds His unique, divine gifts to our natural talents and abilities. When we combine what He gives us with what has already been given to us, and we seek to use both our natural gifts and the gifts of the Holy Spirit for the Lord's purposes, we are serving God with the whole heart, mind, and soul, and we will be the most effective in our contributions to God's kingdom.

∽ What natural talents and abilities do you have? How are you using them to serve the Lord?

∽ What natural talents do you see in others around you? How can you encourage them to use them for the Lord?

Gift or Gifts?

The Holy Spirit Himself is the gift of the Father to everyone who believes in Jesus Christ. Paul said to the Corinthians that other believers within the church longed to be with them "because of the exceeding grace of God in you. Thanks be to God for His indescribable gift!" (2 Cor. 9:14-15). That gift is the Holy Spirit, the evidence of God's grace in them.

We receive the Holy Spirit as the supreme Gift, and then He imparts to us of His ability as He wills. We do not receive spiritual gifts apart from the Gift Giver, the Holy Spirit.

The gift of the Spirit is the Holy Spirit Himself. The gifts of the Spirit are the helps, capacities, and endowments that He bestows on us so that we might accomplish His purposes. All of the gifts are the property of the Holy Spirit. We don't own them. We don't create or manufacture them. We don't grow or produce them. They are His gifts to give.

Types of Spiritual Gifts Given to Believers

These spiritual gifts are given to people who follow Christ Jesus. The Holy Spirit does not indwell nonbelievers, so the gifts of the Holy Spirit are not given to those who have not confessed their sins and received God's forgiveness. Three classifications of gifts are made to the believers in the New Testament: motivational gifts, gifts given to the church as a whole, and gifts given for specific situations and circumstances. The Holy Spirit gives these gifts to us at His discretion, but He does give gifts to every believer.

❧ The Motivational Gifts of the Spirit ☙

The motivational gifts of the Spirit are identified in Romans 12:4–8:

> For as we have many members in one body, but all the members do not have the same function, so we, being many, are one body in Christ, and individually members of one another. Having then gifts differing according to the grace that is given to us, let us use them: if prophecy, let us prophesy in proportion to our faith; or ministry, let us use it in our ministering; he who teaches, in teaching; he who exhorts, in exhortation; he who gives, with liberality; he who leads, with diligence; he who shows mercy, with cheerfulness.

Every believer has one of the seven motivational gifts described by Paul. I've listed them with some of the meanings or interpretations of these gifts as they appear in other translations of the Bible:

1. *Prophecy*—forth-telling or the speaking out of God's truth

2. *Ministry*—serving in practical ways (including hospitality and helping)

3. *Teaching*—explaining the Word of God so that others can understand it and apply it to their lives

4. *Exhortation*—encouraging others to follow Christ closely and without hesitation

5. *Giving*—contributing to the needs of others

6. *Leadership*—having the ability to administer, govern, or rule

7. *Mercy*—giving aid to sick and needy persons (including those who have no merit)

Paul also describes the ways in which we are to use the gifts: prophecy—with faith; ministry and teaching and exhortation—with grace; giving—with generosity; leading—with diligence; and mercy—with cheerfulness.

How do you know which of these gifts you have? Examine your life. When a problem arises that you know has a spiritual dimension, what is your first response? Do you immediately want to speak the truth? Do you start to provide help, to give, or to organize others? Do you jump in and act with mercy for people who are hurting? Do you respond with words of encouragement that others stay close to the Lord and obey Him explicitly?

∽ Which of these motivational gifts best fits your personality?

∽ How can you use this gift in the Lord's service?

∽ Gifts Given to the Church ∽

In addition to the endowments that the Holy Spirit gives to individual believers, the Holy Spirit gives gifts to the church as a whole. These gifts are actually people:

94

He Himself gave some to be apostles, some prophets, some evangelists, and some pastors and teachers, for the equipping of the saints for the work of ministry, for the edifying of the body of Christ, till we all come to the unity of the faith and of the knowledge of the Son of God, to a perfect man, to the measure of the stature of the fullness of Christ; that we should no longer be children, tossed to and fro and carried about with every wind of doctrine, by the trickery of men, in the cunning craftiness of deceitful plotting, but, speaking the truth in love, may grow up in all things into Him who is the head—Christ

—Ephesians 4:11–15

The gifts are given to some in the church. They are called to be:

ᔑ *apostles*—those who are trailblazers, leaders of new ministry outreaches.

ᔑ *prophets*—those who tell the truth of God, including the ultimate consequences of following or failing to follow God's will.

ᔑ *evangelists*—those who proclaim the gospel of Jesus Christ and inspire others to believe in Him.

ᔑ *pastors and teachers*—those who nurture, prepare, and teach the believers, equipping them for service to others.

Not every person is called to one of these roles within the church, but ministries within a church tend to cluster around these areas of leadership. For example, you may not be called to be a pastor/teacher to a congregation of people, but you may be called by God to serve as a Sunday school teacher. You are operating in the area of ministry as a teacher to the body of Christ, under the leadership of one who is gifted to lead in that area. Or you may serve on an evangelism team. You are serving in the area of evangelism, under the leadership of one who has been gifted to lead in that area.

You will find great fulfillment serving within the area of ministry to which the Lord calls you. You will find frustration, disappointment, and dissatisfaction in your attempts to serve within an area of ministry to which you are not called by the Holy Spirit.

&. In which area of ministry do you find the Lord leading you with the greatest regularity?

&. How do you feel when you serve in that capacity? How do you feel when you attempt to serve in other areas?

&. Gifts Unique to Specific Circumstances or Times &.

The New Testament provides a third set of gifts given to believers by the Holy Spirit. This set of gifts is unique to particular situations and times. In fact, Paul provided this list because he desired to see order restored to the services in the church at Corinth:

> Now concerning spiritual gifts, brethren, I do not want you to be ignorant.... There are diversities of gifts, but the same Spirit. There are differences of ministries, but the same Lord.

96

And there are diversities of activities, but it is the same God who works all in all. But the manifestation of the Spirit is given to each one for the profit of all: for to one is given the word of wisdom through the Spirit, to another the word of knowledge through the same Spirit, to another faith by the same Spirit, to another gifts of healings by the same Spirit, to another the working of miracles, to another prophecy, to another discerning of spirits, to another different kinds of tongues, to another the interpretation of tongues. But one and the same Spirit works all these things, distributing to each one individually as He wills. For as the body is one and has many members, but all the members of that one body, being many, are one body, so also is Christ. For by one Spirit we were all baptized into one body—whether Jews or Greeks, whether slaves or free—and have all been made to drink into one Spirit.

—1 Corinthians 12:1, 4–13

Paul's primary concern was not with listing gifts, but with the point that there is only one Holy Spirit. The Corinthians had been idol worshipers, pagan Greeks prior to their conversion to Christ Jesus. They had a different god for each activity, enterprise, and object. Athens, for example, was filled with thousands of idols, each with a specific identity and purpose. Some idol gods were more valued than others. Paul wanted the Corinthians to understand that there is only one Holy Spirit—He manifests Himself in different ways through different individuals as He wills.

The gifts that Paul cited are specific to particular times and events. As the church would gather, different gifts might be manifested depending on the needs of the people and the problems in the church at that time. Paul wanted them to understand that all of the gifts come from the same Holy Spirit, with no one gift being the definitive manifestation of the Spirit's presence in their midst.

These gifts are bestowed on the believers so that one person may be given one gift and another person another gift. All of the gifts are possible, but none of them is assured in any one setting or group of people. In like manner, no one person has his or her identity associated with a particular gift. In other words, one person is not expected to be the prophet at all meetings, and another person the one who gives a word of wisdom. The Holy Spirit speaks and works through this one, and that one, and another one at His direction and for His purposes.

The conclusion that we must draw, therefore, is that a believer may experience one or more of these gifts operating through him during his lifetime, but not necessarily with any predictability or regularity, because the Holy Spirit orchestrates His particular set of gifts to be in operation in each group of people depending on the needs in the group.

The Corinthians apparently had a fondness for the more dramatic gifts, such as healing, tongues, and working miracles. Paul admonished them in 1 Corinthians 13 that love is far more important than spiritual gifts, and then in 1 Corinthians 14 he admonished them to desire prophecy as the foremost gift, so that they might speak the truth of God with clarity to nonbelievers and believers alike.

In 1 Corinthians 12:1, 4–13 above, why does Paul frequently reiterate that gifts are "by the same Spirit"?

⚘ What does Paul's metaphor of the Christian body reveal about the gifts of the Spirit? In what ways can a part of your body serve different functions at different times?

⚘ A Unique Blend ⚘

How do all of these gifts fit together for the individual believer? First, you must discern your motivational gift and operate in it. Then, you must follow the leading of the Holy Spirit as He calls you to a particular area of ministry within the church. As you use your motivational gift in ministry within the church, you must continually make yourself available to the Spirit to manifest Himself through you with one or more of the spiritual gifts in 1 Corinthians 12.

God knows who you are. He knows who He created you to be and which natural gifts, talents, abilities, and personality traits He put into your life. He knows which motivational gift is best suited to you. God knows how to place us within a body of people to accomplish His ministry. He will open doors of opportunity for you to minister in a way that is suited to your natural gifts and your motivational gift.

Finally, God knows His master plan for this world and what is needed to fulfill it at any second in history. He knows the people that He needs in which areas of ministry at which times and places, and for which purposes. Therefore, He knows which specific spiritual gift is necessary at any given time for the accomplishing of His purposes. The Holy Spirit is the giver of these gifts, and they are always given at His discretion and for His purposes. Be open to how and when the Holy Spirit chooses to use you.

> Are all apostles? Are all prophets? Are all teachers? Are all workers of miracles? Do all have gifts of healings? Do all speak with tongues? Do all interpret? But earnestly desire the best gifts. And yet I show you a more excellent way.
>
> —1 Corinthians 12:29–31

What is Paul's point in these verses? Why is it important to recognize that nobody has all gifts?

> Though I speak with the tongues of men and of angels, but have not love, I have become sounding brass or a clanging cymbal. And though I have the gift of prophecy, and understand all mysteries and all knowledge, and though I have all faith, so that I could remove mountains, but have not love, I am nothing. And though I bestow all my goods to feed the poor, and though I give my body to be burned, but have not love, it profits me nothing.
>
> —1 Corinthians 13:1–3

When have you seen someone exercise a gift without love? When have you done it yourself? What resulted?

Why is love essential in exercising spiritual gifts? What would each of the above gifts be like without it?

Today and Tomorrow

TODAY: THE LORD GIVES MANY GIFTS TO HIS CHILDREN, AND THEY ARE TO BE USED TO SERVE OTHERS.

TOMORROW: I WILL ASK THE LORD TO SHOW ME THE GIFTS HE HAS GIVEN ME AND HOW TO USE THEM.

LESSON 9

Making Our Ministries Effective

─── ❧ **In This Lesson** ☙ ───

LEARNING: WHAT IS THE PURPOSE OF SPIRITUAL GIFTS?

GROWING: HOW SHOULD I BE SERVING THE BODY OF CHRIST?

⸰❦⸱

In the last lesson, we discussed the unique blend of spiritual gifts that the Holy Spirit bestows on believers in Christ Jesus. In this lesson we are going to focus on the reasons that the Holy Spirit gives us these gifts. There are four main reasons for the bestowal of spiritual gifts in our lives:

1. They are for the common good of all believers.
2. They equip us for further ministry.
3. They are for our encouragement.
4. They are for our edification.

Ultimately, all of the gifts are intended to be manifested so that Jesus Christ is lifted up and God the Father is glorified. Anytime the spiritual gifts call attention to the ones who are manifesting them, we are in error. All spiritual gifts belong to God and come from Him, and all praise should be directed to God for the results or benefits of these gifts.

Furthermore, we are to hold these gifts and to use them as good stewards of God's grace. We are to recognize at all times that we didn't create these gifts or authorize their use, and we have no right to lay claim to them. We are to use them wisely for the purpose that their true owner, the Holy Spirit, intended. The servant may use the master's utensils, china, and silverware to prepare and serve a magnificent meal for the benefit of the master's guests, but the servant does not own the utensils, china, and silverware. In like manner, we employ the gifts of the Spirit for the benefit of others.

This does not mean that we are to take the bestowal of spiritual gifts lightly. We are to cherish them, hold them in high regard, and manifest them in our lives with boldness, confidence, and dignity. Peter wrote:

> As each one has received a gift, minister it to one another, as good stewards of the manifold grace of God. If anyone speaks, let him speak as the oracles of God. If anyone ministers, let him do it as with the ability which God supplies, that in all things God may be glorified through Jesus Christ, to whom belong the glory and the dominion forever and ever.
>
> —1 Peter 4:10–11

The gifts that we receive from the Holy Spirit are for us to use for the benefit of others. Freely we have received of the Spirit, and freely we give. (See Matt. 10:8.) What we receive from God we are expected to share with others for their benefit more than for our benefit. We, in turn, receive from others the benefit from the gifts that the Holy Spirit gives to them. In this way, we are formed into a body of believers and are built up as a community of faith.

☙ What does it mean to minister "as with the ability which God supplies"? How else might a person minister to others?

103

≈ How might spiritual gifts be misused to serve oneself instead of others? How might the praise and honor be misdirected?

For the Common Good

The gifts are to be used "for the profit of all" (1 Cor. 12:7). When one hurts in the body of Christ, all are hurt. When one is blessed, all are blessed. The gifts are intended to bring healing, wholeness, and benefit to a body of believers. The motivational gift that you receive from the Holy Spirit is given *to* you, but it is *for* others. (See Rom. 12:4-7—prophecy, ministry, teaching, exhortation, giving, leadership, mercy.) If you are given a role in the church, your ministry gift is for service to others. (See Eph. 4:11—apostle, prophet, evangelist, pastor, teacher.) If you are given a spiritual gift, you are to manifest it and help others. (See 1 Cor. 12:7-10—word of wisdom, word of knowledge, faith, healings, miracles, prophecy, discerning of spirits, tongues, interpretation of tongues.) Always ask yourself, "How can I use this gift for the common good?"

For Equipping the Saints

Recall that Ephesians 4:11–12 tells us that the gifts to the church—the placing of apostles, prophets, evangelists, pastors, and teachers within the church—are for this purpose: "equipping of the saints for the work of ministry." The purpose of a good sermon is to inspire the congregation to be obedient and faithful in their walk with the Lord. The purpose of a good Bible lesson is to help people grow in faith and in their understanding about how to apply the Bible to their lives.

Paul also wrote to the Ephesians, "We are His workmanship, created in Christ Jesus for good works, which God prepared beforehand that we should walk in them" (Eph. 2:10). You are God's masterpiece. He has saved you, gifted you with natural abilities and talents, protected and provided for you, and now, through the Holy Spirit, He has given you spiritual gifts. At the same time, He has prepared a place for you to use the gifts. Even as the Lord was preparing you to serve in His church, He was preparing others to receive what you have to give. He has paved the way for your ministry to be effective. In other words, others need what the Holy Spirit prompts you to prepare and give to them. You, in turn, need what others have been prompted by the Holy Spirit to give to you.

When we see that every person who crosses our path has been allowed to cross our path by the Holy Spirit, for a purpose that has benefit to us, what a marvelous adventure we experience in daily living! Furthermore, if a believer crosses our path, that believer has been put there by the Holy Spirit for the express purpose of equipping us in some way for the work of ministry. There is something that we are to learn or acquire from every conversation, every encounter, with another saint of God.

 What does it mean that the gifts of the Spirit are for the "equipping of the saints for the work of ministry"?

 When has the Lord brought you together with another Christian so that you could give your gift to him or her? When have you been on the receiving end of this blessing?

For Encouragement of the Believers

We need encouragement in our lives on a daily basis. We need someone to build us up and help us see our value and worth before the Lord.
The devil and the world's systems grind us down and wear us out. We
need others in the body of Christ to remind us that we are God's unique
and irreplaceable creations, called to unique and irreplaceable places
of ministry. We need to be reminded of God's love for us and of our
importance to the church.

Paul addressed this need for encouragement in his letter to Corinth:

> If the foot should say, "Because I am not a hand, I am not of the
> body," is it therefore not of the body? And if the ear should say,
> "Because I am not an eye, I am not of the body," is it therefore
> not of the body? If the whole body were an eye, where would
> be the hearing? If the whole were hearing, where would be the
> smelling? But now God has set the members, each one of them,
> in the body just as He pleased. And if they were all one mem-
> ber, where would the body be? But now indeed there are many
> members, yet one body. And the eye cannot say to the hand,
> "I have no need of you"; nor again the head to the feet, "I have
> no need of you." No, much rather, those members of the body
> which seem to be weaker are necessary. And those members
> of the body which we think to be less honorable, on these we
> bestow greater honor; and our unpresentable parts have great-
> er modesty, but our presentable parts have no need. But God
> composed the body, having given greater honor to that part
> which lacks it, that there should be no schism in the body, but
> that the members should have the same care for one another.
> And if one member suffers, all the members suffer with it; or if
> one member is honored, all the members rejoice with it.

—1 Corinthians 12:15–26

As the gifts of the Spirit are shared among believers, under the direction and orchestration of the Spirit, we can't help having an awareness that God counts each of us as highly valuable in His church. No matter what our social status, profession, or lot in life may be, we can be used by the Holy Spirit in valuable roles of ministry.

You may say, "I don't see how God can use me. I'm totally inadequate." Or you may say, "I can't be used by God. I'll fail." But God says, "Let me use you. I'll use whatever you do and I'll be in whatever you do, and that means that it will be a blessing to someone. I never fail, and since I'm in whatever good you do for My body, whatever you do won't fail."

Your spiritual gifts should always bring encouragement to others. Even if you have a motivational gift of exhortation, the ultimate purpose of exhortation is to say to another person, "You can follow Christ. You can walk in obedience and righteousness before Him." If you operate in the gift of evangelism, exercise your gift so that people hear the good news that Jesus came to save them from their sins, not that a hell is waiting to swallow them up. If you give a word of wisdom to another person, that word of wisdom is to give him direction that points him toward God and toward His answers in his life. Such a word will automatically point them away from danger and sin, but it should do so as an encouraging word to receive God's best in his life.

⟳ Which part of your body would you not miss if it were removed? What does this suggest about the need for all believers and all gifts?

◦ God has set each believer to perform a specific function in the body "just as He pleased". What does this suggest about the value of *your* gifts?

For Edification

Spiritual gifts are to be exercised for the edification of the church. *Edification* means the "building up" or the "strengthening" of the church. Paul wrote, "Since you are zealous for spiritual gifts, let it be for the edification of the church that you seek to excel" (1 Cor. 14:12). All things are to be done so that the church body as a whole might be perfected— so that sin might be cleansed from a group of believers, so that healing and wholeness might occur individually and collectively, so that conflicts might be resolved and relationships reconciled, so that losses might be restored and excesses trimmed away.

In writing about the gifts to the church, Paul gave an outline of what edification produces. (See Eph. 4:13-15.) A thoroughly edified group of believers would have this profile:

◦ Unity of the faith and of the knowledge of the Son of God
◦ Manifesting the fullness of Christ
◦ No longer tossed to and fro by the wind of every doctrine that comes to town
◦ No longer deceived by the trickery of men
◦ No longer engaged in deceitful plotting or cunning craftiness
◦ Speaking the truth in love

Paul concluded that the end result of edification is a "whole body"—one that is "joined and knit together by what every joint supplies, according to the effective working by which every part does its share" (Eph. 4:16). As with the manifestation of spiritual gifts, this process is to be marked by love (v. 16).

As you think back over your motivational gifts and your role of ministry within the church, ask yourself, "Am I manifesting the gifts of the Spirit so that the entire body of Christ is built up? Are my gifts contributing toward our perfection as a group of believers in Christ Jesus?"

✑ In what ways do spiritual gifts "join and knit together" the body of Christ? Give specific examples.

✑ What part do you play in your local body of Christians? Are you performing that function fully and willingly?

Lasting Benefits

The gifts of the Holy Spirit bless us now, and they bless forever, when they are manifested in ministry that is for the common good, that equips the saints for further ministry, that is marked by encouragement, and that results in edification. Paul declared to the Corinthians, "We are God's fellow workers; you are God's field, you are God's building." He followed that statement with these sobering words:

> According to the grace of God which was given to me, as a wise master builder I have laid the foundation, and another builds on it. But let each one take heed how he builds on it. For no other foundation can anyone lay than that which is laid, which is Jesus Christ. Now if anyone builds on this foundation with gold, silver, precious stones, wood, hay, straw, each one's work will become clear; for the Day will declare it, because it will be revealed by fire; and the fire will test each one's work, of what sort it is. If anyone's work which he has built on it endures, he will receive a reward. If anyone's work is burned, he will suffer loss; but he himself will be saved, yet so as through fire.
>
> —1 Corinthians 3:9–15

Your use of the Holy Spirit's gifts in ministry is not just for here and now. They should have an eternal ring to them, and they will if they truly are gifts from the Holy Spirit. When you invite the Holy Spirit to work through you to bless others, He will do so. He is eternal, and whatever He does through you will have an eternal quality to it. If you want to minister in effective ways, you must want your ministry to last for all eternity. That can happen only as you allow the Holy Spirit to help you in any act of ministry that you undertake. It can happen only as you regard each spiritual gift as coming from Him and being used for the perfecting of His body.

What sort of ministry will endure the test of fire? What sort of ministry will be burned up?

Will your own ministry stand the test of fire? How can you increase the eternal value of what you do for the Lord today?

Today and Tomorrow

TODAY: THE HOLY SPIRIT'S GIFTS ARE FOR THE BENEFIT OF OTHERS, AND THE RESULTS ARE ETERNAL.

TOMORROW: I WILL ASK THE LORD TO TEACH ME HOW TO PRODUCE FRUIT THAT WILL LAST FOREVER.

LESSON 10

Relying on the Spirit for Daily Guidance

✎ In This Lesson ✎

LEARNING: WHAT IS THE DAY-TO-DAY ROLE OF THE SPIRIT IN MY LIFE?

GROWING: HOW CAN I UNDERSTAND GOD'S WILL FOR ME?

To whom do you turn for daily guidance in how to live your life? The Scriptures tell us that the only Guide worth having in our lives is the Holy Spirit. He is the only One who knows our past completely from the moment that we were conceived to this present day, who knows our future completely, from this day extending into eternity, and who knows God's plan and purpose for us today and each day of our lives.

When we turn to people for advice, we must be aware that in many cases they will tell us only what they think we want to hear. They want to make us feel good so that we will like them more, which in turn makes them feel good. If you seek advice from another person, get advice that is honest, true to God's Word, and without ulterior motive. Even as you receive advice from others, you must check it against the Holy Spirit's witness in your spirit, and against the Bible to verify that the advice is right for you in your given circumstance.

Only the Holy Spirit knows what is fully good and right for you on a daily basis. Any other opinion can be only a part of the full truth, which is known by the Holy Spirit. In John 14–16, Jesus refers to the Holy

Spirit repeatedly as the Spirit of truth. The Spirit of truth is like an inner compass in our lives—always pointing us toward what Jesus would be, say, or do in any given moment or circumstance.

> He will glorify Me, for He will take of what is Mine and declare it to you.

> —John 16:14

≪. What does it mean that the Holy Spirit "will take of what is Mine and declare it to you"? How does this glorify Christ?

≪. According to this verse, why is the Holy Spirit's presence necessary for us to correctly use His gifts?

God Has Always Sought to Guide His People

Daily guidance is not something that was initiated by Jesus in sending the Holy Spirit to us. Guidance has been God's desire for His people throughout the ages. Numerous verses in the Old Testament point toward God's guidance of His people. Certainly, He provided daily guidance for His people as they left Egypt and crossed the wilderness to the land that God had promised to them. His guidance then was manifested as a pillar of cloud by day and a pillar of fire by night. (Recall that the symbol of fire is usually associated with the Holy Spirit.)

The leaders of the early church relied on the Holy Spirit to give them this kind of specific, personal guidance, and we are wise to do likewise. Both Romans 8:14 and Galatians 5:18 refer to our being "led by the Spirit." This is to be the norm of the Christian life.

> Trust in the LORD with all your heart, And lean not on your own understanding; In all your ways acknowledge Him, And He shall direct your paths.
>
> —Proverbs 3:5–6

What does it mean to "lean on your own understanding"? How is this different from trusting the Lord? Give practical examples of each.

෴ What does it mean to "acknowledge the Lord" in all our ways? How is this done?

෴ What Are the Results of His Guidance? ෴

The Scriptures describe at least three wonderful results of the Holy Spirit's guidance in our lives.

1. He will convict of sin, of righteousness, and of judgment (John 16:8). The Holy Spirit gives us a very clear understanding of what is wrong, what is right, and how to tell the difference. He reveals the truth of any situation to us to keep us from stumbling or from entering into error. He truly "delivers us from evil" in this way. (See Matt. 6:13.)

2. He will help us "walk circumspectly, not as fools but as wise, redeeming the time, because the days are evil" (Eph. 5:15-16). He will lead us to right choices, right relationships, and right priorities so that we might enjoy the maximum fulfillment. He will help us to make the most of our time each day.

3. He searches our hearts (Rom. 8:27). He reveals to us our deepest motives and desires.

In so doing, the Holy Spirit shows us who we really are and how we can become more like Jesus. He gives us guidance to help us mature in the Lord and become more like Jesus day by day.

The LORD is my shepherd; I shall not want. He makes me to lie down in green pastures; He leads me beside the still waters.

—Psalm 23:1–2

🙠 What does David mean when he says "I shall not want"?

🙠 Consider the shepherd and sheep imagery in these verses. What do they teach about the Holy Spirit's work in a believer?

Conditions for the Spirit's Guidance

There any some conditions placed upon the guidance of the Holy Spirit in our lives.

First, we must believe in Jesus. We must accept Him as our personal Savior, confess our sins, and receive God's forgiveness. The Holy Spirit does not give daily guidance to nonbelievers. The only direction that the Holy Spirit gives to nonbelievers is the conviction that they need to accept Christ Jesus.

Second, we must stay yielded to the Spirit. We must say yes to the Spirit when He prompts us to take a certain action or say a certain word. We must give mental assent to the Spirit's direction, and we must actually obey His prompting and follow through in doing or saying what He has called us to do or say. You can know that you are yielded to Him when you can say to Him, "Here is what I desire. But if Your answer is no to this, it's all right. I'll do what You say."

Third, we must believe for His guidance. We must expect the Holy Spirit to speak in the inner person and direct us toward good and away from evil. We must be intentional and focused in this. We are much more likely to hear what the Holy Spirit has to say to us if we are actively listening for Him to speak. We are much more likely to see the Holy Spirit's direction if we are looking for His signs. Hebrews 11:6 tells us that God is a "rewarder of those who diligently seek Him." We are to be diligent in seeking His guidance, asking for it, watching for it, anticipating it, and receiving it.

Fourth, we are to wait upon the Lord until we receive His guidance. Psalm 27:14 tells us:

> Wait on the LORD; Be of good courage, And He shall strengthen your heart; Wait, I say, on the LORD!

Until the Lord tells you what role you are to play, don't act. If you don't know what to say, stay and pray. If you don't know where to turn, don't get up from your knees. Don't become impatient in your desire to hear from the Lord—wait and listen. His guidance will come.

∽ What does it mean to wait on the Lord? Give practical examples.

117

☙ When have you rushed ahead of the Lord's guidance? When have you waited patiently? What resulted in each circumstance?

How Guidance Is Imparted to Us

The Holy Spirit imparts His daily guidance to us primarily in these ways:

He speaks to us through the words of the Bible. The Spirit will never lead you to do anything that is contrary to God's Word. If you believe that you have heard the Lord speak in your heart, go to the Word of God to confirm that message. Very often as we are reading God's Word, He speaks in our hearts, "Do this. This is for you. That's My desire for you." He brings certain passages to life for us.

We can always find a phrase or verse in the Bible to back up what we desire to do in our human nature. I am not at all suggesting that you go to the Bible to "get a verse" as justification for the decision that you've already chosen to make. That's not being led by the Spirit. Rather, I'm recommending that you read your Bible daily with this prayer on your lips: "Holy Spirit, speak to me through the Word. Just as You inspired men of old to write these words, inspire me to apply these words to my life."

He gives us the principles of the Word of God to guide us in making decisions. In many cases, there isn't a specific story or passage of Scripture that seems to speak directly to our situation. But the principles of God's Word are true and eternal. They can be applied to give us guidance in making choices and decisions.

Ask yourself these questions: "Will God be glorified in this?" "Can I give thanks to God for this?" "Can I do this in the name of Jesus, fully expecting His blessing, His provision, and His stamp of approval?" If you can answer yes to these questions about a decision that you are about to make, you are making your decision within the principles of God's Word.

> And whatever you do in word or deed, do all in the name of the Lord Jesus, giving thanks to God the Father through Him.

> —Colossians 3:17

∽ What does it mean, in practical terms, to "do all in the name of the Lord Jesus"?

∽ Why are we commanded to give thanks to the Father even when we are serving Him?

He speaks to us through circumstances. As we wait upon the Lord and trust Him for guidance, the Spirit very often opens certain doors in our lives and closes other doors. "All things work together for good to those who love God, to those who are the called according to His purpose" (Rom. 8:28). We should remember that all the circumstances of our lives are under God's direct sovereignty, and He allows things to happen for His own purposes.

He speaks to us in the stillness of our hearts with a word of conviction or assurance. When the Holy Spirit is directing us away from something harmful to us, we very often have a heaviness or a feeling of trouble, foreboding, or uneasiness in our spirits. When the Holy Spirit is directing us toward things that are helpful to us, we tend to feel a deep inner peace, an eagerness to see what God will do, and a feeling of joy.

❧ A Complete Guidance ❧

The Holy Spirit often works predominantly through one of these methods to give us guidance, but His complete guidance is usually confirmed as He uses *all* of these methods to speak His truth to us. We read something in the Word that speaks to us. We are reminded of general principles in God's Word, and we begin to see how they apply to our situation—perhaps through the message of a song or a sermon, the words of a friend, or a sudden recollection of passages that we have read in God's Word previously. We see circumstances beginning to change around us. We feel the presence of the Spirit in our lives convicting us to turn from evil or His assurance that we can embrace fully something that will be for our good.

The Holy Spirit does not want God's will for our lives be a mystery to us. He has come to reveal the truth to us. He has come in His all-knowing ability to impart to us what we need to know in order to live obedient and faithful lives. Trust Him to guide you, now and always!

Be anxious for nothing, but in everything by prayer and supplication, with thanksgiving, let your requests be made known to
God; and the peace of God, which surpasses all understanding,
will guard your hearts and minds through Christ Jesus.

—Philippians 4:6–7

❧ Why does Paul command us not to be anxious? How does our
own will influence anxiety?

❧ Why does Paul add "with thanksgiving" to our prayers and
supplications? Why is it important for us to be thankful to God?

My Final Word to You

The Spirit-filled life. I opened this Bible study with those words, and I want to close with them. But let me add the word *wonderful* to this phrase: *the wonderful Spirit-filled life.* The life that the Holy Spirit desires to impart to you can be described only as wonderful—wonderful in the many benefits that we experience personally; wonderful in the many blessings that come to others around us; wonderful in the sense that we are made more keenly aware of the glory and majesty of God the Father and Jesus Christ, His Son. The Spirit-filled life should be marked by awe that we should be so privileged as to be indwelled by the Holy Spirit of almighty God, who desires to use us in accomplishing His purposes on earth and who desires to live with us forever in eternity.

The extent to which you live a Spirit-led life is up to you. Choose today to rely on the Holy Spirit for every aspect of your life, in every decision or choice that you make, during every hour of every day. Trust Him to work through you. Trust Him to mold you into the image of Christ Jesus. Trust Him to bless you as you have never been blessed before. As you ask Him to do His work in your life, you will receive His help and guidance. And in the process, you will manifest His character.

Your ears shall hear a word behind you, saying, "This is the way, walk in it," Whenever you turn to the right hand Or whenever you turn to the left.

—Isaiah 30:21

What major insights have you gained in your study of the Holy Spirit?

Where is God guiding you today? How has your relationship with His Spirit helped you to understand His leading?

~ Today and Tomorrow ~

TODAY: THE HOLY SPIRIT WANTS TO GUIDE ME INTO GOD'S COMPLETE PLAN AND IMAGE.

TOMORROW: I WILL MAKE MYSELF FULLY AVAILABLE TO FOLLOW AND OBEY THE HOLY SPIRIT.

∽ **Notes and Prayer Requests:** ∽